AAK- 9641

Science of Coaching

BASEBALL

Science of Coaching Series

Jerry Kindall, MA
Head Baseball Coach and Associate Professor
University of Arizona

Editor

Leisure Press
Champaign, Illinois

Library of Congress Cataloging-in-Publication Data

Science of coaching baseball / editor, Jerry Kindall.
    p.   cm. -- (Science of coaching series)
    Includes bibliographical references and index.
    Contents: Motor learning / Craig A. Wrisberg -- Sport psychology /
Tom Hanson -- Biomechanics / Lois Klatt -- Exercise physiology /
Coop DeRenne -- Sports medicine / Herb Amato -- Nutrition / Gale
Beliveau Carey.
    ISBN 0-88011-402-9
    1. Baseball--Coaching.   2. Baseball--Psychological aspects.
    3. Baseball--Physiological aspects.   I. Kindall, Jerry.
    II. Series.
    GV875.5.S36   1992
    796.357'07'7--dc20   90-28366
                                      CIP

ISBN: 0-88011-402-9

Acquisitions Editor: Brian Holding
Developmental Editors: June I. Decker, PhD,
   Robert King, and Lori K. Garrett
Assistant Editors: Dawn Levy and
   Elizabeth Bridgett
Copyeditor: Wendy Nelson
Proofreaders: Terry Olive and
   Julia Anderson
Indexer: William O. Lively

Production Director: Ernie Noa
Typesetter: Angela K. Snyder
Text Design: Keith Blomberg
Text Layout: Denise Lowry
Cover Design: Keith Blomberg
Cover Photo: Wilmer Zehr
Illustrations: Dick Flood and Tom Janowski
Printer: Braun-Brumfield

All chapter opener photos are provided courtesy of the University of Tennessee Sports Information Office.

Leisure Press books are available at special discounts for bulk purchase for sales promotions, premiums, fund-raising, or educational use. Special editions or book excerpts can also be created to specification. For details, contact the Special Sales Manager at Leisure Press.

Printed in the United States of America

10 9 8 7 6 5 4 3 2 1

Leisure Press
A Division of Human Kinetics Publishers, Inc.
Box 5076, Champaign, IL 61825-5076
1-800-747-4457

Canada Office:
Human Kinetics Publishers, Inc.
P.O. Box 2503, Windsor, ON N8Y 4S2
1-800-465-7301 (in Canada only)

UK Office:
Human Kinetics Publishers (UK) Ltd.
P.O. Box 18
Rawdon, Leeds LS19 6TG
England
(0532) 504211

Contents

Preface

Over the past 20 years there has been a proliferation of baseball instructional books, videos, tape cassettes, and other "how to" items for coaches in our eager pursuit to be more effective on behalf of our players. Thanks to these much-needed aids, there is little excuse for a baseball coach not to be proficient in teaching the hit, run, throw, and field fundamentals of this great game. Yet few can demonstrate even basic competency in three scientific fields: biomechanics, exercise physiology, and sport psychology. Add to these the mysteries of proper nutrition, motor learning, and sports medicine, and the baseball coach may well feel overwhelmed.

Take heart, Coach! *Science of Coaching Baseball* is a breakthrough for many of us. This book provides working knowledge of the scientific principles underlying successful baseball-team performance. Many coaches avoid trying to apply biomechanics, for instance, in their practices simply because they do not understand the terminology, much less the principles. This book is intended to demystify the "scientific approach" to baseball and give you the confidence to teach heretofore untapped keys to better performance.

Science of Coaching Baseball is certainly not superficial; yet it is not complex. The chapter authors have fully explored the principles and theories of their particular areas of expertise, but they have written in lay language that will ring true to the careful reader. We have carefully developed text and accompanying charts, graphs, headings, and so forth to allow quick understanding and application by coaches. Be assured that this book avoids clichés, elitism, and profundities. Instead you will find a down-to-earth application of the scientific foundations of coaching baseball.

If there is a prevailing characteristic by which I want my own team, the University of Arizona Wildcats, to be recognized, it's the execution of sound baseball fundamentals. I am convinced that these fundamentals can be sharpened and improved by a careful reading of this book. I commend the chapter authors for bringing to the baseball coaching community—from Little League to the major leagues—an extremely helpful resource for improved performance.

Jerry Kindall
University of Arizona

CHAPTER 1

Motor Learning: How to Teach Skills

Craig A. Wrisberg
The University of Tennessee

With spring it comes, as it has come so many springs before. The promise of nail-biting victories. The clutch hit. The roar of the crowd. The sights, sounds, and smells of baseball. In the distance you see them, and the faint sound of ball popping in glove mingles with the friendly chatter of anxious prospects anticipating another season. As you approach the group, you have in your head images of what you would like to see happen this year. Most of all you want to teach fundamentally sound mechanics and smart, heady play.

Your mind wanders as you envision a key game late in the season. Your team is in the field. There's one out in the eighth inning. The tying run is on third base, and the potential winning run is on first. You decide to play your infield in at the corners and halfway around short and second. You know that

1

your infielders must make split-second decisions if the ball is hit to them. They must first determine whether it's hit hard enough to turn a double play. If it isn't they must decide whether to throw home to cut down the tying run or get the force-out at second to keep the potential lead run out of scoring position. You have drilled your players on situations just like this in practice, but now it's up to them to get the job done. You hear the crack of the bat and see a sharp ground ball headed for right field. With sudden sureness your first baseman thrusts out his glove hand to stab the ball and in one smooth motion delivers a chest-high throw toward second base. Your shortstop catches the ball, moves across the bag while eluding the sliding base runner, and makes the return throw to first. Your pitcher, who has broken to cover the bag as soon as the ball is hit to the right side of the infield, catches it in stride and, running parallel to the foul line in fair territory, beats the runner to the base to complete a nifty 3-6-1 double play. They did it! Your kids rose to the occasion, and you're proud of them.

Suddenly your mind snaps back to the present, and you realize that this kind of dream will come true only if you prepare your players properly during preseason workouts. You are also aware that you only have so much time during each practice session, and you find yourself wondering whether you're doing enough to get your players ready for the demands of competition.

As you think about your practice sessions you conclude that you're doing the kinds of things most coaches do. You start with a warm-up period of throwing to loosen up the arm. Then comes batting practice, beginning with a few bunt attempts and continuing for however many swings you decide on for that day. The rest of the time you focus on infield drills while your outfielders and pitchers shag fly balls. You usually follow this with a more organized round of fielding and throwing and perhaps a few game situations. Finally, you conclude practice with wind sprints or some other running activity. Afterward most of your players take off, although one or two might ask to stay for extra batting or fielding, or occasionally a pitcher will want to do some additional throwing or perhaps work on his pickoff move.

On the surface, this practice format seems adequate to you. You've done it this way for years, and it's gone OK. Yet you sometimes find yourself wondering whether there's anything else you could be doing to improve the quality of your team's workouts. That's because you care about your athletes and want to offer them the best experience possible during the time they will be playing for you.

I'm not sure who first coined the expression, *It's not practice that makes perfect . . . it's perfect practice that makes perfect,* but whoever it was realized that the preparation of athletes for the demands of competitive sport requires a practice routine that involves more than just going through the motions. To most coaches this means an emphasis on the principles that have stood baseball's test of time—like watching the ball all the way into the glove, getting set before you throw, or knowing what to do if the ball is hit to you. However, there is also a good deal of information from the field of motor learning that you may want to consider as you go about deciding how to best organize and conduct your team's practice sessions.

The object of this chapter is to present a variety of concepts and principles from the scientific literature in motor learning that are relevant to the learning of baseball skills and strategies. Some of the concepts discussed may already be familiar to you, although you might not have thought about them in the way they are presented. You might be like the batter who thinks he is watching the ball until someone asks him if he has ever noticed the seams. Regardless of your familiarity with it, the material in this chapter is meant to help you improve the quality of your practice sessions in important ways that will prepare your athletes for the many and varied challenges found in the game of baseball.

First, the concept of motor learning and its importance to you as a coach is explained. Then a number of motor learning concerns are discussed. This is followed by a section offering more specific suggestions and examples of ways you can put motor learning to work for you. Finally, a number of keys to success are listed to help you maximize the learning experiences of your players.

WHY MOTOR LEARNING IS IMPORTANT

The term *motor learning* simply refers to issues and questions dealing with the learning of movements. For example, what are the mental and physical demands your players face when they try to master the movements of baseball (catching, throwing, batting, baserunning, sliding, etc.)? Or how might your practice sessions be structured to promote the most effective and efficient skill development? Answers to these and other questions are available in the motor learning literature.

The performance of most baseball skills depends on a player's ability to size up a situation and respond appropriately. Take the task of batting, for example. Before each pitch the batter must note the alignment of the defense, remember the game situation (the number of outs, the count, the number and location of runners on base, etc.), and correctly interpret signals from the base coach. As the pitch is delivered the batter must visually focus first on the point of release and then on the speed and rotation of the approaching ball, decide whether to take the pitch or attempt to hit it, and, if it turns out to be a swing, deliver the head of the bat into the hitting zone at exactly the time and place at which the ball arrives. Like most tasks in baseball, this one requires at least three types of attention, involving picking up important information in the environment (e.g., the rotation on the ball after it leaves the pitcher's hand), deciding what to do (e.g., to hit an outside pitch in the hole between first and second), and correctly executing the desired movement (e.g., the right-handed batter keeping the hands out in front of the bat head until contact with the ball occurs).

Every task your players perform involves various amounts of each of these types of attention, and often their decisions must be made very quickly. To be successful, they must learn to anticipate the important aspects of each situation and devote their attention only to those things that will result in correct responses. Your understanding of this conceptual framework from the field of motor learning as well as other principles discussed in this chapter will enable you to help your players master the fundamental skills of the game and compete successfully.

MOTOR LEARNING CONCERNS IN BASEBALL

In this section a number of motor learning concerns are discussed along with general suggestions for how to deal with them.

What Individual Difference Factors Affect Performance and Learning?

Each of your players is unique and is influenced by different things. There are several factors that may affect how well your players learn and perform baseball skills.

Abilities

If you've coached for any length of time, or if you haven't coached at all but know something about baseball skills, you have probably noticed that players on most teams differ in the abilities they bring with them to the practice field. To take advantage of the abilities players have or to provide opportunity for players to overcome their deficiencies, you must first identify the abilities required for successful performance and then structure practice sessions so that these abilities are either improved upon or reinforced.

In Table 1.1 a sample scorecard is presented for you to use to rate the abilities of each of your players. Perhaps you can think of other abilities to add to this list. The important thing to remember is that abilities such as these play important roles in promoting (or impairing, if there are deficiencies) your players' performance. Once you have compiled scorecards for all your players and have reviewed these with them individually, you can refer to them when planning practice activities. Periodic evaluation (e.g., preseason, midseason, postseason) of your players will help you chart their progress. As you notice a player improving in certain areas, you can update his scorecard and begin introducing him to more advanced practice experiences.

Attention and Memory

Every one of your players is limited in his capacity to attend to or remember things. In fact, the average person can probably handle no more than five to nine pieces of information in a single dose. By "handle" I mean give conscious attention to. The implication for you as you plan practices or prepare your players for game situations is to emphasize only a few things at a time. This means you have to decide which two or three tips, cues, or bits of information are the most important for your players to try to focus on or remember at any one time.

You may also need to direct different players' attention to different things, depending on their abilities or past experiences. More experienced players will be better able to devote their attention to cues in the environment, because they are probably capable of performing their movements without consciously attending to them. Therefore, you might remind an experienced player to "get the force-out at second if there is no play at the plate" but may need to instruct a beginning-level player to "charge a ground ball and keep your glove down." The most important point for you to remember is that players will only be able to concentrate on a few (usually the fewer the better) things at a time, so you must limit the amount of information you give them.

Arousal Level

Ideally, you would like each of your players to approach practices and games with the proper intensity. What "proper" means is sometimes difficult to put your finger on, but you are probably aware that there is some "ideal" level of arousal or mental readiness necessary for the successful performance of any task. You don't want your players to fall

Table 1.1
A Sample Abilities Scorecard

Player's name _____

Date _____

Skill	Rating	Comments
Throwing		
Multilimb coordination of arms and legs	_____	_____
Arm and wrist speed	_____	_____
Accuracy	_____	_____
Power	_____	_____
Catching		
Eye–hand coordination	_____	_____
Clear vision	_____	_____
Eyes on ball	_____	_____
Glove placement	_____	_____
Hand quickness	_____	_____
Anticipation and timing	_____	_____
Hitting		
Eye–hand coordination	_____	_____
Multilimb coordination of arms and legs	_____	_____
Clear vision	_____	_____
Eyes on ball	_____	_____
Speed of reaction	_____	_____
Power	_____	_____
Arm and wrist speed	_____	_____
Bat control	_____	_____
Anticipation and timing	_____	_____
Baserunning		
Total body coordination	_____	_____
Foot speed	_____	_____
Quick start	_____	_____
Speed of reaction	_____	_____
Eye–foot coordination	_____	_____

1 = Poor, 2 = Below average, 3 = Average, 4 = Good, 5 = Excellent, NA = Not applicable.

asleep (i.e., be underaroused) on the field, but you also hope they won't "play tight" (i.e., be overaroused) (Figure 1.1). Factors to consider in helping your players achieve the right level of arousal include the personality makeup of the player, the demands of the task, and the amount of

Figure 1.1 The effects on performance of too little, too much, and just-right arousal.

pressure the player is feeling in a given situation. Generally, the more anxious a player tends to be, the more difficult the task he must perform, and the more pressure he feels in a situation, the more likely his arousal level will be too high for optimal performance, resulting in errors of commission (e.g., swinging at a pitch over his head, throwing to the wrong base). In cases like this you need to help the athlete reduce his arousal level. On the other hand, the less anxious a player tends to be, the simpler the task he is asked to perform, and the less pressure he feels in a particular situation, the more likely his arousal level will be too low for optimal performance, resulting in errors of omission (e.g., letting a routine ground ball go through his legs, taking a called third strike down the middle of the plate). In cases like this you need to help the player increase his arousal level.

It is important to realize that arousal level may also influence a player's attention. This means that if he is either underaroused or overaroused, his attention will tend to either drift off or be occupied with irrelevant information. Overarousal may further reduce a player's limited attentional capacity, and information that is normally handled with ease may suddenly seem complex and overwhelming.

It would be useful for you to consider whether your players' arousal levels are appropriate for the tasks and situations the players must face. You might also ask yourself whether you have any players on your team who seem to be consistently underaroused or overanxious in practice or games. An overanxious player might feel that the things he is being asked to do are too difficult for him. Or he might feel that others (including you) will think less of him if he makes a mistake. In either case you are in a position to help lower that player's arousal level by asking him to do only those things he feels confident in doing and by letting him know that you

Figure 1.2   Use encouragement rather than criticism when your players make mistakes.

appreciate the effort he gives regardless of whether he makes a mistake or not. For this type of player, praise is almost always more effective than criticism (Figure 1.2).

Motivation

Another aspect of a player's frame of mind is his level of motivation. If you are like most coaches, you may be most concerned about motivation when working with athletes. You probably often find yourself wondering why some players are so excited about what they are doing while others couldn't seem to care less. Or perhaps you have been puzzled by the fact that a particular player appears to be highly motivated on one occasion and completely disinterested on another.

In all likelihood a player's level of motivation is influenced by the extent to which he feels his needs are being met in a particular situation. For example, when a player with a strong need to achieve success is provided with opportunities to excel on the baseball field, he will probably exhibit more motivation than if he does not have sufficient opportunity to perform well. You can usually motivate this type of player by adding competitive situations to practice sessions.

It would probably be useful to ask yourself why you think each of your players wants to be on the team. In Figure 1.3 a number of incentives that have been reported by athletes to be important reasons for their involvement in competitive sports are shown. As you can see, being part of a group (affiliation) and the opportunity to demonstrate performance excellence (excellence) are among the strongest incentives for many players. Moreover, it is clear that athletes are usually motivated by realistic challenges (stress).

The key point to remember is that your players may have different reasons for participating. So, if you can determine which incentives are

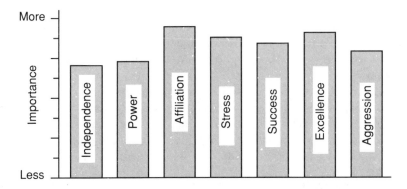

Figure 1.3 Motivational incentives of athletes. *Note.* From "An Analysis of Incentive Motivation in Young Canadian Athletes" by R.B. Alderman and N.L. Wood, 1976, *Canadian Journal of Applied Sports Sciences*, **1**, p. 171. Adapted by permission.

the most attractive to each of them and then provide them with opportunities to experience those incentives during practice and games, you will probably not have to worry as much about their motivation.

What Are Some Task and Environmental Factors That Affect Performance and Learning?

There are several external factors that will influence how your players learn and perform their baseball skills. You should consider each of these when you plan your practice sessions.

Difficulty of the Task

In determining the best approach to the practice of various tasks, you will need to consider how difficult each task is. Although the level of task difficulty is largely a matter of the performer's perceptions, there are a few objective guidelines for evaluating the difficulty of tasks. For the most part, tasks with a number of component parts or information-processing demands are going to be more difficult. Consider, for example, a first baseman's task during a 3-6-3 double play. The ball must be fielded cleanly, an accurate throw must be delivered to second base, a quick retreat must be made to the first-base bag, and a successful catch of the return throw from the shortstop must be accomplished. It is obvious that this task has a number of components and a variety of attention demands. The first baseman must visually track the ball as it comes off the bat, accurately read the speed and bounce of the ball, anticipate the time and location of its arrival, cleanly field the ball in the catching hand, transfer it to the throwing hand, deliver an accurate throw to second base that is easy for the shortstop to handle and does not hit the base runner, move quickly to the first-base bag, and successfully catch the return throw from the shortstop.

If you sense that a task like this is too difficult for a particular player to practice as a whole, you could break it down into parts and have him practice them separately. When determining what constitutes a part, be sure to keep together components of the task that are highly related. In the case of the 3-6-3 double play, you would probably want to combine fielding of the ground ball and throwing to second as one part and re-treating to the base and catching the return throw as another. As soon as a first baseman demonstrates successful mastery of the separate parts of the task, you should combine them and give him experience with the whole sequence. Occasionally you may feel it is necessary for a player to go back to the practice of one or more parts, but usually when whole-task practice has been successfully mastered it should be employed. And of course, simpler tasks (e.g., throwing) or those requiring a quick coordi-nated action (e.g., the pop-up slide) should always be practiced as whole movements. Your job is to determine the level of difficulty of the various tasks you expect your players to perform and, for those that must be broken down into parts, make sure that the different parts contain compo-nents that go together.

Predictability of the Environment

Another factor you should consider when attempting to structure practice experiences for your players is uncertainty in the environment in which the task is to be performed. For many baseball skills, learning them re-quires that the player be able to successfully predict or anticipate events going on around him. For example, an outfielder who wants to put him-self in the proper position to catch a fly ball must carefully watch the ball to anticipate where and when it will come down. Similarly, a successful batter observes the movements of the opposing pitcher, as well as the flight path of the approaching ball, to predict what type of pitch it will be, how fast the ball is moving, and whether the ball will be in the strike zone when it crosses the plate.

Given our earlier discussion of individuals' limited capacities to process information, it may be necessary for you to determine whether environ-mental uncertainty should be reduced to give your players a better chance for success. For example, if your catcher is having difficulty handling the low pitch that bounces in the dirt, he might not have learned to recognize the way different pitches (e.g., fastballs, sliders, curveballs) react when they bounce. If so, you could make the practice environment more pre-dictable by throwing him only one type of pitch (e.g., fastballs) until he consistently demonstrates an ability to block it or keep it from getting away. Then you could move to another type of pitch (e.g., curveballs) until he begins to get the feel for how it reacts in the dirt. This exercise could be repeated using each of the pitches he must learn to deal with. Once your catcher masters the task of blocking each type of pitch in isolation, you could reintroduce environmental uncertainty by mixing up the pitches. Perhaps nonbreaking pitches (fastballs and change-ups) could be combined first. In this way the catcher would be required to make slightly more difficult predictions about the relative speed of pitches yet wouldn't have to be concerned about the possibility that they would be breaking (as would curveballs, sliders, etc.). By gradually introducing more variety into the practice situation you would be building your catcher's confidence in handling any type of low pitch in a game situation.

More detailed discussion of things you can do to help your players deal with uncertainties in the baseball environment will be presented later in this chapter. For now it is important only that you understand the potential impact of environmental uncertainty on the performance of your players and begin to think of ways you might manipulate the environment to enhance skill acquisition.

Attention Demands of Tasks

Given the fact that attention is limited, it is important for you to identify the types of demands contained in each task you expect your players to perform. Successful determination of specific attention demands allows you to direct your players' focus to those aspects of a task that promote correct performance. In this section, examples of the three general categories of attention demands are given.

Receiving Information

This type of demand is present whenever something happens in the environment that affects the way information is received. Examples include weather-related phenomena such as sun in the eyes, wind, dust, or a "high sky," as well as factors that compete for the player's attention, such as the presence of important friends in the audience or a "herky-jerky" motion by an opposing pitcher. In short, this type of demand is a potential threat to your players' abilities to clearly pick up the most relevant environmental information. In some cases the problem can be solved by the use of proper equipment (e.g., sunglasses) or by teaching players to focus on task-relevant cues (e.g., the approaching pitch) (Figure 1.4) and ignore irrelevant stimuli (e.g., people in the crowd). Other times little can be done, as with unpredictable changes in wind direction during pop flies. Whenever possible, try to identify things that may affect your players' abilities to pick up important information and then assist players with techniques for dealing with each.

Figure 1.4 A fielder with eyes focused on the ball.

Making Decisions

Assuming that your players are able to adequately pick up important cues, the challenge for them becomes one of interpreting this information and determining the most appropriate responses. Examples of decisions that must be made include a batter determining that a pitch is breaking away and deciding he will try to hit it to the opposite field, or a first baseman deciding whether to go after a ground ball hit to the right side of the infield or to retreat to the bag. For the most part a player's ability to make accurate decisions improves with increased experience under gamelike circumstances. An experienced batter who has seen numerous speeds and breaks of pitches delivered by different types of pitchers in a variety of past situations is more likely to correctly identify the speed and break of the next pitch. This is in part due to the fact that he has learned to anticipate what certain pitchers are likely to throw in specific situations (which is probably why experienced batters sometimes report having more difficulty with pitchers they have never faced before). To facilitate this capability in your less-experienced batters, you should expose them to a wide variety of pitches and pitchers during practices. The more at-bats they get against different pitchers, the better they will become at anticipating, reading, and reacting to the pitch. Allowing them this opportunity in actual games may be frustrating for you at first, but increased exposure to competition will only serve to improve their decision-making skills and increase their chances of making good contact.

Performing the Movement

Execution of a mechanically correct movement contains demands of its own. For example, a center fielder must determine where and when in his throwing motion he should release the ball to deliver it on a line toward home plate so that it may be cut off or be easily handled by the catcher. You can help your players produce an accurate movement by relating it to similar ones they may have performed in the past or by providing them with familiar images. For example, the center fielder practicing an overhand throw might be instructed to release the ball at the two-o'clock position or as his hand passes over the top of his head (Figure 1.5). A pitcher might be told to release a change-up in a fashion similar to that involved in pulling down a window shade. A batter might be instructed to slow down his body and speed up his wrists. For images or cues to be effective, they must be ones players can relate to. And remember that images that work for some players may not be beneficial for others.

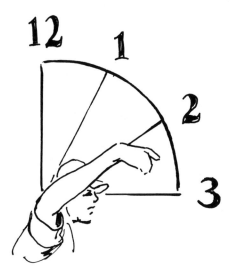

Figure 1.5 A player performing a throwing movement with an image of the two-o'clock position for the release point.

PUTTING MOTOR LEARNING TO WORK FOR YOU

This section is designed to help you put motor learning to work for you. Specific suggestions are offered to help you identify the components and attention demands of each of the tasks you want your players to perform, gain and focus your players' attention, structure the practice of different tasks, provide demonstrations and feedback, and help your athletes practice smart.

How Do I Classify the Tasks My Players Must Perform?

To answer this question you must think about the fundamental components of the tasks. Most popular books on the coaching of baseball provide detailed explanations of the mechanics of the various skills of the game (batting, throwing, catching, baserunning, etc.). If you have coached for some time you could probably write down your own list of components. In Table 1.2 sample task components for the skills of batting and throwing, as well as those for the more specific task of stealing second base, are given. In teaching these components to your players you will find that some things require more detailed explanation than others. For

Table 1.2
Analysis of Baseball Tasks

Task	Component	Importance[a]
Batting	Grip	7
	Stance	8
	Position of hands	6
	Eyes on ball	3
	Decision to swing	4
	Stride	2
	Swing	1
	Follow-through	5
Throwing	Grip	7
	Stance	3
	Balance	2
	Take-back	5
	Throw	1
	Follow-through	4
	Recovery	6
Stealing second base	Stance	6
	Balance	1
	Eyes on pitcher	2
	First step	3
	Running	8
	Approach to base	5
	Slide	4
	Recovery	7

[a]The most important component is given a rating of 1; the next most important component is rated 2, etc.

example, the batting grip can usually be explained and checked fairly easily, but the swing itself may demand more focused instruction, experience with a variety of practice situations, and more specific performance feedback.

How Do I Determine the Attention Demands of Tasks?

Once you have defined the fundamental components of the tasks, you should identify the attention demands associated with each. That way you will have a constant reminder of the things that will require most of your players' attention. In Table 1.3 possible sources of attention demands associated with each of the fundamental components of batting are presented. Although it is probably true that some amount of each type of demand is contained in each component, only the most significant types of demands are indicated in the table. For example, the decision to swing at a pitch or take it will be primarily determined by how well the batter sees the ball (receiving information) and reads its speed and direction (making decisions). On the other hand, the major demand of the swing itself will be in the production of a mechanically correct movement (performing the movement). Since performers' attention is limited, you may sometimes need to reduce the demands of some components in order to allow your players to focus on others.

It is very important that players' attention be directed to the most important information they need to work on at any particular time. If a batter

Table 1.3
**Attention Demands Associated With Each
of the Fundamental Components of the Task of Batting**

	Type of demand		
Component	Receiving information	Making decisions	Performing the movement
Grip			X
Stance			X
Position of hands			X
Eyes on ball	X	X	
Decision to swing	X	X	
Stride			X
Swing			X
Follow-through			X

is having difficulty determining whether or not to swing at a pitch, his attention might be directed to the tasks of observing the angle of the pitcher's arm, watching the ball as it leaves his hand, and determining its speed and type of spin. To sharpen your batter's attention to the ball you might have him stand in the batter's box and just watch pitches thrown at different arm angles, release points, speeds, and spins (receiving information). After some period of time is spent watching, the batter could be asked to identify pitches and state how he would respond to them (making decisions). Was it a slider or a curveball? Did the pitch break down, or was it flat? Would you try to pull it or hit it to the opposite field? When demands associated with performing the movement (e.g., striding, swinging, and following through) are minimized, the batter's attention is more fully devoted to reading and deciding what to do with the pitch. A good time for a player to do this during a game would be in the bull pen with pitchers who are warming up.

In the same vein, if a batter's swing is choppy, the proper stride, swing, and follow-through could be practiced by having him hit balls from a tee or from a ball machine set to deliver pitches at a constant speed to a fixed location. Once the swing mechanics are smoothed out, the demands of watching the ball and timing its arrival could be reintroduced by having the batter respond to a variety of pitches. At this point he should be able to devote most of his attention to reading the pitch and deciding what to do with it, because he is capable of performing the swing more automatically.

How Can I Get My Players' Attention?

In order to assure that your players are ready to deal with the various demands of different tasks, it is important that you first secure their undivided attention. Never waste practice time trying to talk to your athletes when they do not appear to be attending to what you are saying. Some things attract people's attention more than others, but there are a few general rules to keep in mind to maximize the chances of gaining your players' attention. First, try to communicate things that are meaningful. Nothing is more meaningful to people than their names, and you can almost always get a player's attention by speaking his name. Meaningfulness is also related to tasks a person is expected to perform. For example, outfielders are more interested in information that will help them catch fly balls and make accurate throws to bases than they are in techniques for fielding a sacrifice bunt. Therefore, you should make sure that the information you give to any group of players is relevant to them.

Because vision is the dominant sensory system, a second rule for gaining attention is to take advantage of visual cues or aids whenever possible. Demonstrations that are eye-catching will more likely get the attention of your players than will lengthy verbal explanations. More detailed discussion of ways to provide helpful demonstrations is given later in this chapter.

A third general way to gain your players' attention is to occasionally do something unexpected. A sudden loud noise or a change in practice routine are applications of this rule. The former example should not be overdone, but it can be effective from time to time. To change practice routine, you might have outfielders and infielders switch defensive positions or hold a short scrimmage in which batters hit from the opposite side of the plate than they are used to. Such variations not only serve to combat boredom but often enhance players' appreciation of the demands of their teammates' positions and sharpen their attentional focus.

A final rule for gaining attention is to have specific goals for players to strive for during each practice. If athletes arrive to find only a vague plan or outline for practice, their attention will probably wander and little will be accomplished. So it is important to post a practice plan each day that gives time allotments and players' names for different activities. More detailed discussion of practice plans is provided in the section on practicing smart.

How Can I Help My Players Focus Their Attention?

There are several important types of information that you should direct your players' attention to. One type involves all the important cues that will contribute to successful task performance. For example, if reading the motion of the opposing pitcher is important, reminding your batters to watch his arm motion may improve the speed with which they learn to recognize his pitches. You might want to look at Tables 1.2 and 1.3 again for guidelines as to the important aspects of attention associated with different movement components or tasks. It is also a good idea for players to sharpen their focus on movements they perform during practice. In a double-play situation, a shortstop should try to make his throws to the center of the second baseman's glove rather than just in the general direction of the base. Such experiences will serve to ingrain the correct movement pattern and improve the precision of a player's movements.

A second source of information deserving of your players' attention is a plan of action. Do your batters think about where they will try to hit the ball when they are ahead in the count? Do they look for a pitch in a certain location with the idea of driving the ball in a particular direction? By directing their attention to the development of a specific plan of action prior to movement execution you will be contributing to their performance success. Any time players can plan in advance what they want to do, it will be to their advantage.

A third thing you should occasionally direct your players' attention to is the process of self-evaluation. Encourage them to try to figure out what may have caused them to make a bad throw, miss a pitch, or drop the ball. Players who learn how to evaluate their performance are usually able to focus better on tasks and adapt more readily to new situations. You might even consider the merits of holding a team review session after practices or games. If moderated properly this could be a profitable time of evaluation and information sharing.

Essential to self-evaluation is feedback, which is a fourth type of information you can direct your players' attention to. You might do this by asking a batter to notice how his hands feel after he has executed a successful hit-and-run play or reminding a catcher to think about where in his throwing motion he released a ball that wound up sailing over the second baseman's head and into center field. The key is to determine which sources of information are most important to players at any particular moment and then attempt to direct their attention to those sources.

How Should I Provide Demonstrations and Give Feedback?

One of the more important tasks you are expected to perform as a coach is to communicate information that is useful to your players. You know that their attention is limited and that they must learn to devote it to those things that will result in the best possible performance. In this chapter considerable discussion has been devoted to the various types of attention demands of tasks and to ways you can help your players focus on the most important cues. Two additional situations calling for the provision of information are those involving demonstrations and the giving of feedback.

Demonstrations of tasks or movements can be useful to your players when they are attempting to learn new skills or refine old ones. The idea is to provide a model of correct performance that they can attempt to emulate. When thinking about using demonstrations you should keep a couple of things in mind. First, demonstrations should only portray the correct execution of the movement or task, because that is what your players will be attempting to reproduce. If you are unable to perform the demonstration yourself, ask an experienced player who is respected by his teammates to serve as a model. Second, demonstrations should accentuate those aspects of the task that are most important. This usually means visual cues such as the footwork of the pivotman on a double play. However, it may occasionally involve an emphasis on nonvisual cues, such as the difference in the timing of the sound of the ball hitting the bat when a pitch is being pulled and when it is being hit to the opposite field. In this case the observer would be able to combine the sight and the sound of the ball contacting the bat to get a better idea of the swing's timing.

Feedback is important to learning and performance because it provides the athlete with information he can use to repeat the things he has done correctly, change the things he has done incorrectly, and evaluate the progress he is making toward a goal he may have set for himself. In addition to the things he can see, hear, and feel for himself when he executes a movement, a player will often benefit from information you call to his attention. This could be in the form of a spoken comment (e.g., "It looked to me like your eyes were not on the ball") or a visual demonstration (e.g., showing him how his eyes shifted away from the ball at a particular moment) given immediately after the movement. Or it could mean directing his attention to a particular source of information before he attempts a movement, to impress on him something he might not otherwise pick up. For example, a batter working on improving the mechanics of his swing might be asked to close his eyes to feel what he is doing (Figure 1.6). After he has executed a swing with his eyes closed, you could provide spoken feedback about what the swing looked like. As this exercise is repeated he should begin to appreciate what a correct-looking swing feels like. Finally, remember that feedback can be used to help your players develop the capability to recognize their own mistakes as well as to assist them in learning how to move correctly. To facilitate the development of error detection skills, you should ask your players to tell you what they thought they did wrong before telling them what you saw.

Figure 1.6   Swinging with the eyes closed can help a batter improve hitting mechanics.

How Should I Structure the Practice of Tasks?

It is always important to structure practice sessions in ways that will challenge your players, keep their interest, and maximize the benefits of the activities they are involved in. To achieve this goal several principles should be kept in mind.

First, the amount of time allotted to the practice of a task should depend on how well learned or complex it is. Generally speaking, when a player is trying to learn a new skill or is practicing a more difficult task, he should be given more repetitions of the movement and more time between trials to think about what he is doing or needs to do. However, once he has learned the skill or can perform it with little difficulty, fewer repetitions and less time between repetitions are required.

Second, for the practice of most tasks, short bouts of performance are better than long ones. If players know they have only a few chances to do something (e.g., execute a sacrifice bunt), they usually devote more concentration to the task and are less likely to become bored with it.

Third, practicing a random sequence of movements in a drill sometimes leads to better learning and transfer to game conditions than does performing successive repetitions of the same movement. This is probably because the game of baseball rarely requires a player to do the same thing twice in succession. How often do all fielding attempts a third baseman gets in a game involve ground balls hit right to him at the same moderate speed? When players are required to do something different during each fielding chance in a round of practice, they will probably be more alert and attentive to what they are doing than if they know they will be getting three repetitions of the same thing (e.g., a medium-speed ground ball that is to be fielded and thrown to first base). Variety of practice demands will also help players learn the types of adjustments of basic movement patterns needed for different situations. Outfielders who are required to make throws to second, third, and home from a number of locations and depths in practice will be better prepared to make the mechanically correct throw in a particular game situation. Your job is to come up with creative variations of practice activities for your players and be patient with the outcomes. A variety of demands may result in more errors being committed during a practice session, particularly early in the season, but it will probably pay dividends come game time.

How Can I Help My Players Practice Smart?

An old adage in sports is that "you play like you practiced." If practice is unorganized and piecemeal, players tend to cultivate sloppy habits. There are some things in your players' performance you have little control over, but one thing you have complete control over is practice organization.

How systematic is *your* approach to practice? Do you have a *plan* for the season? For the next game? For today's practice? The most important thing you can do for your players to ensure that they "practice smart" is to have a clearly defined practice plan. This provides focus and goals for your

Table 1.4
A Sample Practice Plan

Date:
Equipment:
Time schedule and practice activities

3:30-3:45	Warm up. 2-3 minutes light jogging 2-3 minutes static stretching At least 10 minutes throwing; more (up to 15) early in season

3:45-4:15	Practice previously taught skills.
	Pitchers, catchers, and first basemen (10 repetitions of each move)
	   Pickoff moves (conventional move and step-off-rubber-before-
	     throwing move; vary time in "set" position)
	Second basemen and shortstops
	   Double play pivots (5 repetitions of each pivot)
	     Shortstop: Brush with right foot; mound side of second; backing
	      off
	     Second baseman: Right foot leap and flip; mound side of second;
	      beyond base on left-field side; backing off
	Outfielders and third basemen
	   Throws to third base (two rounds of 5 repetitions each)
	   Objectives: Throws should be able to be cut off and arrive on one
	     bounce.

4:15-4:20	Water break
4:20-4:50	Learn new skill: the double rundown play. Situation: Runners at first and third. Runner is caught off first, and during rundown runner on third breaks for home. Objective: Retire lead runner. Know your position (throwing, catching, tagging, backing up). Minimize number of throws.
4:50-5:20	Practice under game conditions. Situations: Home team, leading 3-2, top of ninth, runners at second and third, one out Visiting team, game tied, bottom of ninth, bases loaded, no outs
5:20-5:45	Baserunning sprints (first to second, first to third, first to home; 3 repetitions of each) Cool down Static stretching Coach's comments; questions and answers

players and encourages the development of proper habits for them to take into game situations. Players respect an organized coach, and with that respect comes a readiness to learn. A sample practice plan is shown in Table 1.4. Having a specific plan will allow you to evaluate the improvement of your team and determine areas needing further attention.

There are at least three primary features of any good practice plan. First, the plan is simple. Players should know exactly what they are expected to do and not be overloaded with too much information. To keep things simple you must decide which aspects of performance will contribute the most to your players' development.

Second, it is challenging. Good practice plans involve activities that force your players to aim higher and attempt to achieve more. To do that you must be sure to include activities that will stretch and challenge them.

Third, it is gamelike. You should always be thinking about how the activities your players are performing during practice will benefit them in game situations. You should not only include activities that will transfer to the game environment but also point out to your players exactly how the activities apply. Prior to or following certain situations you might ask them to tell you either what they would do or what the basis was for what they did do. For example, after practicing a rundown between first and second base you might quiz your infielders as to what they would do if there happened to be another base runner on third. Decision-making skills can also be improved by directing your players' attention to important events at other times, as when they are sitting in the dugout or standing in the on-deck circle. In fact, you should take every opportunity to encourage your players to observe the important aspects of the game environment.

The development of systematic practice plans that are simple, challenging, and gamelike will offer your players crisp, purposeful training experiences that promote skill development and smart play.

KEYS TO SUCCESS

- **Keep records on the abilities of your players and refer to these to create practice experiences that will facilitate improvement.**
- **Identify the important attention demands of each task.**
- **Remember that you may need to temporarily reduce the attention demands of a task to focus a player's attention on particular cues.**
- **Always direct players' attention to the most important cues of a task.**

- Monitor players' attentional focus by periodically asking players what they are thinking about or what they will be noticing in the next moment.

- Learn to recognize when players are underaroused or overaroused and assist them in achieving optimal arousal for performance situations.

- Identify incentives that are important to each of your players and try to include those incentives in every practice session.

- When breaking a task into parts for practice, keep together components that are strongly related.

- To get your players' attention, keep things meaningful, use variety, and have specific goals for them.

- Encourage your players to think about plans of action for different situations and to evaluate their own performances.

- When demonstrating a skill or giving feedback, provide players with the most important cues or information for learning.

- Before giving feedback about a movement, make sure the player is attending to the same cues you are.

- Reduce the number of repetitions of a movement and the time for reflection between repetitions as players' performance improves.

- To promote learning and transfer to game situations, keep practice bouts short and varied rather than long and repetitious.

- Always have a clearly defined practice plan that is simple, challenging, and gamelike.

RESOURCES

Alderman, R.B., & Wood, N.L. (1976). An analysis of incentive motivation in young Canadian athletes. *Canadian Journal of Applied Sport Sciences*, **1**, 169-176.

Christina, R.W., & Corcos, D.M. (1988). *Coaches guide to teaching sport skills*. Champaign, IL: Human Kinetics.

Fleishman, E.A. (1965). *The structure and measurement of physical fitness*. Englewood Cliffs, NJ: Prentice Hall.

Kerr, R. (1982). *Psychomotor learning*. New York: Saunders.

Magill, R.A. (1989). *Motor learning: Concepts and applications*. Dubuque, IA: Brown.

Marteniuk, R.G. (1976). *Information processing in motor skills.* New York: Holt, Rinehart & Winston.

Salmela, J.H. (1974). An information processing approach to volleyball. *CVA Volleyball Technical Journal, 1,* 49-62.

Schmidt, R.A. (1988). *Motor control and learning.* Champaign, IL: Human Kinetics.

Sports Illustrated book of baseball. (1960). Philadelphia: Lippincott.

Whiting, H.T.A. (1971). *Acquiring ball skill.* Philadelphia: Lea & Febiger.

CHAPTER 2

Sport Psychology:
The Mental Game

Tom Hanson
Skidmore College

It's been a tight ball game from the first pitch. Your team has played well. Your opponent, however, has played just a little better, and after more than two hours of intense baseball you find yourself in a classic pressure-cooker: two outs in the bottom of the ninth, bases loaded, down by one run. The crowd is on their feet, and both dugouts are generating a lot of noise. The opposing coach calls time out to talk to his pitcher, so you decide to have a conference with your hitter, an underclassman you have hitting in the seventh spot in the lineup. Understandably, he looks a little nervous.

What do you say to him? Probably something like "Relax and just watch the ball." But does he have the ability to relax? Has he ever had a chance in practice to be in this situation?

> Does he have a predetermined mental strategy to get his mind ready to hit and help him block out all that noise and pressure?

Clearly, the better you and your athletes are prepared for a situation like this, the better the outcome is likely to be. Helping athletes and coaches successfully prepare for and handle the many mental challenges they face in competition is one of the primary goals of the science of sport psychology.

WHY SPORT PSYCHOLOGY IS IMPORTANT

Few coaches would argue with the notion that psychological factors play an important role in sport performance. In fact, coaches and athletes typically report that anywhere from 50% to 90% of sport performance is mental. Baseball is difficult from a mental standpoint because of the built-in frustrations, such as the difficulty of hitting, the number of things that are beyond an individual's control, and the slow pace of the game. With all that time in between the action, there is plenty of time for negative thoughts to infiltrate the brain.

Despite its importance, most coaches spend surprisingly little time or effort developing the psychological skills of their athletes. Coaches who do not make the effort to develop their athletes' mental abilities leave the mental aspects of the game to chance, adopting an "Either they got it or they ain't" approach. Given the role psychology plays in baseball performance and the recent knowledge that has been generated in sport psychology, this approach is unwise and unnecessary.

SPORT PSYCHOLOGY CONCERNS IN BASEBALL

So much of coaching involves psychology that it is difficult to think of an aspect of coaching where it does not come into play. Psychology has an important role in understanding the importance of such things as your coaching philosophy, how you communicate with your players, how you motivate your players, and what and how you choose to teach them.

For your athletes, sport psychology concerns issues such as motivation, developing consistency, coping with stressful situations, recovering from mistakes, dealing with the frustration that is so inherent in the game, and generally performing to the best of their abilities. A growing awareness of the importance of these aspects of the game have resulted in an ever-increasing number of professional teams seeking the help of sport psychologists to enhance their players' performances.

One other very important sport psychology concern in baseball is coaches' and athletes' views on sport psychology itself. It is important to realize that just like all of the other sport sciences, sport psychology has no magical answers that can guarantee championships or make all of your players pro prospects. There are no substitutes for physical ability and hard work. What sport psychology does do, however, is help give each coach and athlete his best chance of performing as well as he possibly can. Thus, while it can make no great promises, sport psychology should be a high priority for all coaches interested in being successful.

The first part of this chapter addresses what is perhaps the most important aspect of coaching: creating a team atmosphere conducive to successful play. A team's atmosphere, or chemistry, encompasses many things—the feelings the team members have for each other, the morale of the team, communication on the team, the team's motivation to succeed, and so on. A team's atmosphere, then, profoundly affects how successful that team will be. "Successful" here should be taken as meaning more than just winning games. Having fun, learning important lessons for life, and striving to perform to the best of one's ability are a few of the many other things that make a team successful.

In this chapter, a coach's influence over his team's atmosphere will be discussed in terms of the following three general areas: (a) the coach's coaching philosophy, (b) his ability to communicate, and (c) his ability to motivate his players. Certainly many things that affect your team's atmosphere, such as the psychological makeups of your players, are outside of your control, but using some of the suggestions presented here can help you take as much control of your team's atmosphere as possible.

What Is a Coaching Philosophy?

In baseball, most people think of a coach's philosophy as the way he plays the game or his team's style of play. Does he bunt a lot, hit and run a lot, use the squeeze play, or wait for the three-run homer? Certainly these are part of a coach's philosophy, but there is much more to it.

A coach's philosophy involves his attitudes, beliefs, and values. It determines the perspective he takes on all events and people around him, and defines what he thinks is important. Thus, a coach's philosophy impacts everything he does, from how hard he works in the off-season to improve his club, to how he organizes practice, to how he handles a player who has just broken curfew. It influences decision making, how ballplayers are treated, and the consistency with which actions are taken.

A big part of your coaching philosophy involves the way you handle the power inherent in your position. As a coach, you have a great deal of power over your athletes. It is important to realize that not only do your actions and decisions have an impact on your players' experiences in baseball (e.g., do they play, do they learn, do they have fun), but you also have an important influence over their self-esteem or their sense of self-worth. Many athletes erroneously base a great deal of their self-esteem on their baseball performance. Thus, depending on how highly a player regards you, hearing positive or negative comments such as "I'm really pleased with your effort," "You look good out there," "You're terrible," or "I can't trust you out there" can significantly affect a player's self-image. A player's evaluation of himself as a worthy individual is the most important judgment he will make in his lifetime, so the importance of being aware of your power cannot be overemphasized. Thus, whether or not a young man enjoys baseball or "builds character" by playing it depends largely on how you handle your power.

What would you say is your coaching philosophy? Many coaches never take the time to think this through. Because it has such a tremendous

---

GAINING AWARENESS OF YOUR COACHING PHILOSOPHY

The best way to become more aware of your coaching philosophy is to answer some important questions: Why did I originally go into coaching? Why am I still coaching? What are my objectives for my coaching? What do I like about coaching? What do I dislike about coaching? Why do I think the young men on my team play baseball? Is this my team or their team? Do I handle all of my players (starters, nonstarters) in a consistent manner? Which do I put first, the well-being of my athletes or winning? Your answers to these questions go a long way toward defining your coaching philosophy.

Now, consider the following possible objectives of coaching: winning, fun, development of athletes as people, attention directed toward you, money, your athletes' health, being as good a coach as possible.

Certainly, all of these are important. But which are most important to you? Go back over these objectives and rank them in order of importance to you.

It is very easy to rank these objectives. It's another matter to actually behave consistently with the ranking you give them. Think about some of the difficult situations you faced in the past year. Were your actions consistent with the ranking you just gave? If so, great, keep it up. If not then you've identified something to think about and work on.

impact on all aspects of your coaching, though, being aware of your own coaching philosophy is vital to becoming an effective coach. Taking the time to write out answers to the accompanying questions will help you define your coaching philosophy.

What Else Can I Do to Help My Team's Atmosphere?

Another way a coach can enhance his team's atmosphere is to take a positive approach to coaching. Little support can be found in the sport psychology literature for the notion that a coach should be harsh with his players, use a lot of punishment, or scare them into performing for him. That just does not lead to successful performance or satisfied, happy baseball players.

Two major elements contribute significantly to having a positive approach to coaching. The first involves the extensive use of positive reinforcement. Research has found that positive reinforcement, or rewarding players for desirable behaviors, is one of the most basic and yet most powerful tools a coach has. Positive reinforcement not only serves to help your team's atmosphere, but it is also a highly effective means of boosting an athlete's self-confidence level and performance.

Positive reinforcers can be anything the athlete finds rewarding and will increase the probability that he will try to repeat the action that got him the reinforcement. Examples of reinforcers range from smiles and pats on the back to T-shirts and being able to scrimmage after working hard for the first part of practice.

One thing that can make your verbal positive reinforcement more effective is to make it as specific as possible. For example, you give your athlete more information about his performance if you say "Nice job of getting your glove out in front of you, Richie!" instead of just "Nice job, Richie." Also, you can use praise to make an athlete more attentive to an instruction or criticism by occasionally "sandwiching" the instruction between two positive reinforcers. For example, "Your balance looked good all through the delivery, Keith, but you need to follow through a bit farther. Keep working hard, you're looking better." Remember, the praise on either end can be verbal or nonverbal.

The second part of having a positive approach is having fun. Your players' primary motivation to be out there is to have fun, so don't deprive them of it. In addition, there is clearly a strong circular relationship between fun and success: The more fun athletes have, the more successful they tend to be, and the more successful they are, the more fun they tend to have. Researchers aren't sure which comes first, but given the strong relationship between success and fun, coaches interested in being successful while at the same time enhancing their athletes' motivation for playing baseball would be wise to continually help (or at least let) their players have fun. Examples of how to help your players enjoy playing include occasionally letting players play other positions during batting practice, letting pitchers take batting practice, and playing soccer or ultimate frisbee for the day's conditioning. Other good ideas for making your players' baseball experience more enjoyable and bolstering your team's spirit can be obtained simply by asking them about it. Remember, they are the ones out there playing the game, so they are a great and important source of information on all aspects of the game. Don't think that you have all the answers.

How Can I Communicate Better With My Players?

Communication is another important aspect in the creation of a ball club's atmosphere. If you think about it, coaching is communicating (Figure 2.1). A coach's philosophy determines how and what decisions are made and what is emphasized in practices and games, but his ability to communicate with his players determines the way he is perceived by his players. A coach may have a great philosophy and know the game inside and out, but if he is not a good communicator, he is not a good coach.

Figure 2.1   Good communication is an essential coaching skill.

A good communicator is someone who is effective at both getting the information that is in his head into the heads of his players and at the same time letting his players get what is in their heads into his. In other words, communication is a two-way street. Although each coach will be unique in the way he communicates with his players, coaches will be most effective if they follow a few basic communication absolutes.

Sending Messages

Most coaches talk a lot. The good ones, though, actually say a lot. Your goal when talking to your players should be to send understandable messages that are high in information. That is, your players should have no trouble interpreting what you said because you were specific, complete, and direct in your statement, and they should benefit from what you said because it has some meaning or is of value to them.

For example, when talking to a player who is inquiring about his lack of playing time, you could say, "Well, we think you have some ability, so keep working hard, be dedicated, and you never know what might happen," but a much better response (provided it is true!) would be, "In my eyes Mike is ahead of you right now. You need to work on your quickness in the field and make more consistent contact at the plate in order to see more action." The second response is direct and gives the player some concrete information, whereas the first in noncommittal and vague. One effective way to check to see how understandable a statement you just made was is to get feedback from your players. Simply ask them if they understood, or better, have them repeat what you said and then *really listen* to what they say.

Also, when talking to your players as a group, arrange them so that you are sure they all can hear and see you (the dugout doesn't work too well; in front of the dugout or in the outfield is much better). Finally, during a game, don't yell technical instructions out to your players all the time. Because a baseball game has a lot of time when the ball is not in play, it is very easy to continually shout instructions (especially mechanical pointers) out of the dugout or from your coaching box and overload your players with information. Try not to do this—players hate it.

Receiving Messages

How good a listener are you? Many opportunities to help athletes are lost because coaches don't make the effort it takes to listen to what their players have to say. Listening may be the most important part of communicating, and yet our listening skills typically pale in comparison with our ability to talk.

Clearly, the most important point to improving your listening skills is to *want* to listen. To do this you must be motivated to help your athletes as human beings as well as baseball players. Increasing your awareness of the need to listen can instantly make you a better listener. Other helpful hints for being a better listener include making good eye contact with the speaker and facing him squarely (Figure 2.2).

Figure 2.2   Show that you want to listen.

A big step toward becoming a better listener can be taken by engaging in active listening. Essentially, active listening involves paraphrasing what you think the speaker said. In other words (to paraphrase that), instead of simply telling the speaker whatever comes to your mind, reflect back to the speaker your interpretation of what he said. This keeps you mentally involved in what the speaker is saying so your mind doesn't wander. Examples of lead-ins to paraphrase statements include these: "So you're saying that . . . ," "Do you mean that . . . ," "Let me see if I got this right . . . ." This technique is especially helpful when discussing a problem or complicated issue. Try this technique 5 to 10 times today, and see how people react when they realize you are really listening to them.

Nonverbal Communication

Another overlooked aspect of communication is nonverbal communication. Over 50% of all information that is exchanged is transmitted via nonverbal means. If you are in the third-base box with your head down or shaking in disgust, that can have the same effect on a player as a 5-minute verbal chew-out session—both of which may wipe out his confidence. If you have your arms crossed and don't make eye contact with a player, he knows you are not listening to him. On the other hand, if you smile or pat him on the back, he knows you feel good about him. Think of it this way—you know you can tell a lot about a player by the way he acts, so you should realize that you are sending nonverbal information to your players whenever you are in their sight.

Try to be more aware of the nonverbal messages you are sending. Pay attention to things like how you stand, the gestures you make, and how or when you touch any of your players. It is important to show them that you are confident and cool under pressure—this will help them be likewise. If you really want to learn a lot about what your players are seeing when they look at you, have someone videotape you during a ball game or practice.

How Can I Increase My Players' Motivation?

One adjective almost always used when describing a successful individual or team is *motivated*. As a coach, you know what motivation is and how important it is to your team's atmosphere and success, so let's get right to describing some of the ways sport psychologists have determined that coaches most effectively motivate their athletes.

Have Fun

Coaches tend to be motivated primarily to have a good team. Athletes, however, are generally motivated by two things: to be good at their sport and to have fun. Many coaches make the mistake of thinking that it is not possible to both have fun and be good. However, as discussed earlier, the more enjoyable an athlete perceives baseball to be, the harder he will work to become better at it and the more motivated he will be for the team to be successful. This is not to say, of course, that your practices should be earmarked by frivolity. It does mean that you should make it a top priority for your players to enjoy coming to practice and games.

Encourage Player Input

Another way to enhance the motivation of your team is to allow the players to have some input into what happens on the team (team rules, what goes on at practice, where to eat on the road, etc.). Meeting regularly with the seniors or co-captains to get their input on practice and game activities is one good way to foster the leadership that is so important to your team's success. The more they feel it is *their team,* the more effort they are likely to put out to make it successful. Letting the players have input into team rules, for example, can make the rules easier for you to enforce; if a player breaks curfew, it will be his own rule that he broke, not one forced on him from above. Finally, you do not need to implement all of their suggestions; simply giving them the opportunity to express their ideas is highly motivating.

Gain Respect

Thirdly, the amount of respect athletes have for their coach is one of the strongest determiners of how motivated they will be to perform well for him. Clearly, the old adage is true that respect must be earned, it does not come with the position. Coaches can gain the respect of their players by being knowledgeable about the game, being fair and consistent in their handling of their players, and communicating directly and openly with their players (e.g., letting them know their status on the team, explaining lineup changes).

Set Goals

One of the techniques most frequently employed by coaches and sport psychologists to enhance motivation is goal setting. A great deal of information has been published on goal setting, so it will not be addressed at length here. However, one area where coaches often make the mistake of not using goal setting is during practice. Encourage your players to set a specific goal or two before each practice to help keep them from just going through the motions. Examples of good daily practice goals include taking 5 minutes of fungoes at game-level intensity, pitching three innings in the bull pen without walking a batter, hitting three balls up the middle on this round of batting practice, and each player walking away from practice knowing that he worked hard all day.

How Can I Help My Players Be More Confident?

Most athletes and coaches feel that confidence is the name of the game in any sport, and baseball is no exception. "This game is a game played with confidence because this game is played with your head," Met pitcher Ron Darling has said (Dorfman & Kuehl, 1989, p. 104).

College baseball players interviewed in a recent survey said approximately 80% of their performance was determined by their confidence level, or how much they believe in themselves. Clearly, if a baseball player doesn't believe that he is good, all the technical ability in the world will not make him a good player.

When a baseball player has confidence, he does a lot of things right. He does the things he needs to do to play well, he feels great, and he thinks about playing great. The confident player trusts his ability, has control of himself, has all positive images in his head, is thinking all positive thoughts, is relaxed, is paying attention to what he needs to be, and is mentally prepared to play.

But for most players, confidence is as hard to hang on to as a good knuckleball. Rarely does an athlete have everything going just right. Clearly, baseball is a game where players need to be constantly adjusting their mental and emotional levels. Players too often make the mistake of simply letting their performance or how they happen to feel that day dictate their confidence level. Although past performance seems certainly to be the most powerful determiner of a player's confidence level, there are many other methods of increasing confidence levels—it doesn't have to be left to chance.

As a coach, developing the confidence level of your ballplayers should be one of your top priorities. Two questions should continually run through your head: How does what I'm having him do or what I am saying to him affect his confidence? and What could I do to help this guy believe in himself more?

So what can you do to help your players get their hands on this elusive commodity and make the mental adjustments that are so often needed?

At least three ways to build confidence have already been discussed. One of the most powerful means of helping confidence is simple positive reinforcement. Repeatedly praising an athlete for his efforts and telling him that he is a good player will help his confidence. Don't overdo it, though, or your praise will lose its meaning. Also, your modeling confident behavior (e.g., being poised and self-secure after your team makes a crucial error in the last inning) can have a profound effect on your athletes' confidence levels. Remember, confidence is contagious. Thirdly, helping your athletes meet challenging goals they set for themselves can boost their confidence. The following sections discuss several more tools for helping athletes be more confident and make the mental adjustments necessary to maximize performance.

Being Successful

The most powerful tool for building confidence is for an athlete to be successful. Getting base hits leads a hitter to believe in himself, fielding ground balls helps build a player's confidence in his defensive ability, and getting batters out makes a pitcher confident.

Unfortunately, the player has to do these things on his own. As a coach, however, there are some things you can do to help your athletes experience success:

- Be a good coach. Constantly look for ways to get better.
- Define success in terms of things the athlete has control over, such as his effort, and reward him accordingly.
- In practice, simplify drills as much as necessary to let a struggling player experience at least some success.
- Set up your game schedule to give your team a good chance of being successful early in the season.

Learning to Trust

Having confidence could be described as trusting your body. A confident hitter sits back and trusts that his hands will come through in time for him. The nonconfident hitter thinks about his hands and lunges out at the ball early. Similarly, the confident pitcher trusts his body as he goes through his motion so he stays fluid and in control. The nonconfident pitcher doubts himself and is inconsistent and wild. Trusting your body means getting your mind out of the way so your body can do what you've trained it to do. The time for thinking about mechanics or anything other than the task at hand is in practice and perhaps shortly before performing. Come performance time, an athlete needs to "free himself up" and trust his body.

You can help your athletes develop their abilities to trust their bodies by discussing with them what it means to trust one's body and incorporating it into your practice and game-day vocabulary. Hitters need to stay back and trust their hands instead of jumping out at the pitcher, and pitchers can be reminded that they've worked hard on their mechanics and now they need to let go of their mechanical thoughts and trust their bodies—allowing their bodies to throw the ball instead of trying harder.

Keeping Control

To successfully build and maintain confidence, a player must realize what he can and cannot control in a ball game. Other players' performances, bad hops, umpires' calls, line drives hit right at a defender, and so on are all outside of a player's control, so he must not let them have a negative effect on his performance. The only thing that a player can control is himself.

Because each athlete has only the capability to control himself, it is important that he have as much control over himself as possible. Oftentimes, though, ballplayers don't do a very good job of this. How many times each game do you see a batter not have control of himself and swing at a pitch way out of the strike zone, or a pitcher "squeeze the ball" out on the mound?

Common examples of players letting things outside their control negatively affect their performance are pitchers getting upset after a fielder's error or a cheap base hit, and hitters starting to press after a few line-drive outs. It is easy to say "Don't let it bother you," but it is a very difficult thing for a young athlete to do. You can help your athletes by repeatedly emphasizing the importance of focusing on only those things over which they have control and by teaching them the following techniques.

Selective Perception

Selective perception is a psychologist's way of saying, "Look at things in a way that helps you the most." For example, if a batter had a great day today, he needs to focus his thoughts on the immediate past, the things he did today. But if a batter is struggling lately, he needs to spend his time thinking about some time when he was hot, and not on what he's done lately. Of course, much can be learned by analyzing mistakes and being honest about what a player needs to work on, but good players always look at things in ways that will help their confidence, not bring it down. This is another technique you can help your athletes develop by discussing it with them and focusing your conversations with them on their best performances.

Acting Confident

One great and easy way to build confidence is to act confident. Do the things that a confident player does. Constantly showing a confident posture, walk, and manner can do great things for an athlete, because just as a person's thinking greatly influences what he does, likewise what he does influences what he thinks! Thus, acting confident can make an athlete think and feel confident. In addition, it can also undermine the confidence of his opponent!

The most important part of the body to keep in mind here is the sternum, or chest. When a player loses confidence, his body sags and his shoulders droop. The first thing he needs to do is get his sternum up. Try to stick out your chest and feel weak and unconfident—it's hard! So tell your athletes that no matter what happens during the game they should get their sternums up. This is a great one for you to remember, too, Coach.

Visualization

Confident athletes have positive images of themselves in their heads. They are constantly seeing themselves being successful in their "mind's eye." Purposely creating images in your head to build confidence and enhance athletic performance is called visualization, or imagery, and it is one of the most widely used sport psychology techniques.

The reason visualization can be effective is that the mind does not distinguish between what is real and what is only imagined. Getting lost in a fantasy about winning a championship and finding your heart pumping rapidly is a good example of this, as is waking up in a cold sweat after dreaming of forgetting to bring your uniform to an away game. Visualization thus enables athletes to mentally rehearse their performances beforehand, making the athlete more comfortable and confident when it comes time to actually perform.

Most great athletes report using visualization in some way to help their performance. Roberto Clemente, for example, recommended that any time a player made any type of mistake, he should replay the action in his head seeing himself make the play successfully. That way, the last image in your head is a positive one, not a negative one.

As a coach, you want to have your players see themselves do great things in their heads over and over. Not simply daydreaming, though, but conscious, purposeful imaging. In other words, a player needs to visualize specific situations, like particular pitches coming in, facing certain batters, fielding a tough backhander, and anything else that might happen in a game. One of the most common uses of visualization is as a mental preparation strategy. Ballplayers can get themselves ready to play by mentally rehearsing how they want to play during that day's game and how they will handle certain situations.

Visualization can also be used to mentally rehearse successfully coping with negative events such as making an error or giving up a home run. Special visualization audio tapes that guide players through various situations greatly facilitate players' use of this technique and are available commercially (see Ravizza, 1988).

HOW TO USE VISUALIZATION ON GAME DAY

Pitchers:

1. In the dugout between innings, mentally review the hitters coming up in the next inning.
2. Just before the beginning of the windup, see the ball go right to your target.

Hitters:

1. Before the game or when on deck, get into your stance and see the ball come inside, then down the middle, and then outside; and take a swing to pull, go back up the middle, and the other way with the ball, respectively.
2. Study a pitcher warming up and imagine what it will look like to face him, with particular emphasis on identifying his release point.

Fielders:

1. Between pitches, picture the ball being hit to you on the ground, in the air, to your right or to your left, and your fielding it successfully.
2. During pregame, imagine the fungoes you take are live and that a runner is sprinting down the line to first.

Finally, you can facilitate your players' use of visualization by incorporating the basic idea into your daily coaching language. Here are some examples:

"Go over in your mind now what you want to accomplish out on the mound today. See yourself working the different batters."

"Without actually doing it, see if you can get the feeling of your arm coming through in that good slot we've been working on."

"At this hitting station take 50 dry swings, pretending there are different pitches coming in at different locations. Really try to see that ball coming in and then going back out for a line-drive base hit."

"OK, guys, take a minute here and see yourself being on the bus on time tomorrow."

Self-Talk

The words and phrases going through your head (like the words you are now reading, for example) are what is called your self-talk. Everyone engages in self-talk. If you are thinking, you are, in effect, talking to yourself.

The content of the words you say to yourself is of paramount importance. What you say to yourself largely determines your self-confidence, your self-esteem, and how you look at the world. For example, if a hitter constantly tells himself that he is horrible, he will be. If a pitcher tells himself he's great, he may well be. The brain is like a computer: It puts out only what you put into it.

Normally, we are not aware of this running monologue we carry out. This is certainly fortunate—we would go crazy if we constantly thought about thinking. This means, though, that the hitter who is telling himself he is horrible may not realize that by doing so he is sabotaging his own efforts to improve. Thus, because our self-talk plays such an important role in determining our confidence, it would be wise to be aware of it so that we are sure we are saying the right things to ourselves at the right time. That is, we need to be saying the things that will give us the best chance to be successful.

The way self-talk can be used by your players to their advantage is simple: They need to figure out what they say to themselves when they are playing well, or what they would like to say to themselves, and simply say it over and over.

If they can't think of what they say, or if they say they don't say anything, ask them what they think they would be saying if they were talking to themselves. Common phrases are "Nobody can hit me," "I've got good stuff today," and "I can rip this guy." Great players constantly bombard themselves with positive, confidence-enhancing self-talk.

You (and your players) might ask, "What good is it to say these things if you don't really believe them?" Good question! The good answers are these:

1. Saying positive things to yourself is the first step to gaining confidence. Sort of "fake it 'til you make it."

2. It keeps you from saying negative things to yourself. Too many times players sabotage themselves by "beating themselves up" mentally. This only makes things worse.

Relaxation

One of the most prominent characteristics of a confident player is that his movements are relaxed and smooth. Most players, in fact, will tell you that when they are at their best they feel relaxed and fluid. On the other hand, the nonconfident player is typically overly tense and jerky. Although certainly some level of muscle tension is required for optimal performance, too much tension is a ballplayer's worst enemy.

Muscle tension is a natural reaction to a stressful situation. It's the body's way of getting ready for action. However, when an athlete is uptight or stressed out, he hinders himself in two ways: (a) He tenses muscles that are not needed for the movement he is making—like tensing your biceps when you are swinging a bat, working against yourself—and (b) he tenses all his muscles beyond the point needed for efficient movement.

Unfortunately, players often have more tension than they need when performing—especially when the game is on the line. Fortunately, though, there are several simple techniques for helping athletes relax.

The most important technique for relaxation is deep, slow breathing. Telling your players to "take a deep breath out there!" is excellent advice, but only if you have previously discussed with them how it should be done. The procedure is simple: Slowly inhale until your lungs are full, being careful not to raise your shoulders while doing so. After a brief pause, slowly exhale, letting the air come out at its own rate—don't force it out, but let it all out. Let your shoulders drop into a more relaxed position, and slightly extend the exhale, as this is the time when the relaxation occurs (Dorfman & Kuehl, 1989). To be sure the breath is taken slowly enough, count to 3 seconds on the inhale and 4 seconds on the exhale.

Attentional Focus

Regardless of how confident a ballplayer is, if he is not focusing on what he needs to be focusing on, his performance will suffer. A player performing at his peak is totally focused on his target (the catcher's mitt, the pitcher's release point, or the bat meeting the ball), and his mind is free of distracting or irrelevant thoughts. In particular, no thoughts about the past (e.g., "I can't believe Brian made that error") or future (e.g., "I'll bet coach takes me out if I don't get this guy out") enter his mind.

Thus, it is important to identify and discuss with your players what they need to focus their attention on at each moment during the game. The ball, the mitt, a cue phrase such as "just react to the baseball," or whatever.

ON-THE-FIELD RELAXATION TECHNIQUES

1. Take a short break: Take a walk around the mound or step out of the batter's box and tie your shoe.
2. Talk out loud to yourself: Use a slow, gentle tone.
3. Use movement: Moving or stretching your body through long, slow patterns can help recognize and reduce excess tension. For example, the shoulders can be loosened by pushing them forward and back.
4. Visualize: Imagine yourself at some favorite tranquil spot such as a beach or your own bedroom.
5. Tense your muscles for a few seconds, then let them go and focus on the relaxed feeling: Many players will squeeze the ball or bat tightly, then relax their hands to get the feeling they want. (Dorfman & Kuehl, 1989)

This brings up one of the most important aspects in the psychology of baseball: Playing the game one pitch at a time. Although this is always done physically, it is rarely done mentally. Playing one pitch at a time means having one's mind totally focused on the present pitch and not letting thoughts of the results of previous pitches or batted balls interfere with the task at hand (Figure 2.3).

Playing the game one pitch at a time, always focused on the present task, sounds easy, but it is extremely difficult. In his recent book, Orel Hershiser (1989) emphasized that playing the game one pitch at a time is vital to success in pitching. Interestingly, he also said that he did not learn to do it effectively until he was in the big leagues.

Constantly emphasizing to your athletes the importance of playing one pitch at a time is the first step to helping them do so. A second is teaching your players to combine their deep breathing with self-talk to create the simple but effective strategy called focusing. To focus, the player takes a good, deep breath as described earlier, but at the end of the exhale he utters a self-talk statement to encourage himself or remind himself of what he needs to focus on. For example, a pitcher might take a long, slow breath and near the end of the extended exhale say to himself, "One pitch at a time, Mark, just you and the mitt." A hitter's might be, "This pitch, just see the ball and react," and a fielder's, "This one's coming to me." Any self-talk that is encouraging or reminds the player what he should be focusing on is fine, but the player himself should come up with the phrase or phrases he thinks will be most helpful to him. This procedure can be used anytime, and should be used at critical times such as

Figure 2.3   Pitchers should get off the mound and take a good, deep breath when trouble starts.

the start of a new inning, or just after a key event such as an error, giving up a home run, a questionable umpire call, or taking a swing at a very bad pitch.

One great way to help develop your players' abilities to be focused in practice is called *focused catch*. Ken Ravizza (1986) suggests that when playing catch, instead of letting your players' minds (and mouths) wander, have them practice concentrating by trying to hit a specific spot on their partner such as a shoulder or a knee. You can tell who is concentrating by watching where their balls are going.

Routines

Another means of helping a ballplayer prepare his mind for action and play the game one pitch at a time is the use of a preperformance routine. Most good baseball players have some type of routine they use to mentally prepare themselves for competition (Figure 2.4). Wade Boggs, for example, is well known for his elaborate pregame and pre-at-bat routines, which include running at a certain time before the game and executing a certain list of actions before stepping into the batter's box. A routine typically consists of some combination of thoughts, such as self-talk and

Figure 2.4 Batter on deck simulating being up as part of his routine.

imagery, and actions, such as relaxation and stretching. It functions as a funnel, channeling otherwise random thoughts, feelings, and actions into the thoughts, feelings, and actions that the athlete wants to have just prior to performing. Ideally, your athletes are "unconscious" when performing. A good preperformance routine prepares an athlete's mind to do just that.

A routine need not be fancy or complex. In fact, the simpler the better. For example, using the focusing procedure presented earlier before each pitch could be considered a routine. To develop a routine, or to improve one a player already uses, the player should determine what he thinks he should do, think, and feel just before performing. Again, this basically means coming up with a combination of the techniques described earlier that the player feels will best get him ready to perform.

Also, a player may incorporate an "awareness checklist" in his routine, in which the player asks himself the following questions: Am I breathing as deeply as I want to be? Are my muscles as loose as I want them to be? Is my self-talk what I want it to be? Do I have the positive images in my head that I want to have? If the answer to any of these questions is no, the player needs to use the techniques described earlier to make the adjustments necessary to give himself his best possible chance to succeed.

PREPERFORMANCE ROUTINES

Pregame routine:

1. Before getting to the park, spend 10 minutes visualizing what you want to accomplish or have happen during the game.
2. When putting your uniform on, go through a short list of self-talk statements such as "I'm going to be in control of myself all day," "I'm excited and confident about today's game," or "My school-work and outside life are now set aside, it's time to play baseball."
3. Stretch out with the team and then play "focused catch" to prepare your mind to be focused during the game.
4. Go through your awareness checklist to make sure you are feeling as energized but relaxed as you want to be.

Pre-at-bat routine:

1. In the hole: Swing a weighted bat and go through your awareness checklist to spot excess tension or negative thoughts.
2. On deck: Simulate being up to bat by setting up in the box, using focusing procedure, and visualizing the pitcher throwing to you, paying special attention to locating his release point. Go through steps 1 and 2 briefly if you are leading off an inning.
3. Stepping in: Use focusing procedure with the self-talk phrases "see the ball and react" or "right back at him."

Prepitch routine (pitcher):

1. Evaluate your last pitch and remind yourself of any adjustments necessary (e.g., to keep your elbow up), including physical tension levels.
2. Turn attention to the next pitch. Use the act of stepping on the rubber as a cue to focus totally on your catcher and this next pitch.
3. Make a commitment to throw the pitch you've decided on (no doubts or second guesses).
4. Take a deep breath to relax and focus.
5. Go.

Prepitch routine (fielder):

1. After each pitch, take a good breath, stand up, and relax.
2. Think about the situation: "What should I do if it's hit to me?"
3. Remind yourself that you expect each pitch to be hit to you and that you want it to be hit to you.
4. When the pitcher steps on the rubber, pound your mitt with your throwing hand to signal yourself to focus in on the next pitch.
5. React.

So What Is My Objective in Teaching Them All of This?

The bottom line in all of this is that your objective as a coach is to help each athlete get into the proper mindset for performing. For the pitcher, this means being committed to the pitch he is going to throw (no doubts about pitch selection), being totally focused on his target, and being certain that the ball is going to go there. For the hitter, this means being totally locked into seeing the baseball and being certain that he is going to hit it hard. For the fielder, this means focusing on the ball, knowing what he'll do if it's hit to him, and hoping that it is.

As basic as these mindsets sound, they capture the essence of what the mental game of baseball is all about. If each of your athletes could get into these mindsets for every pitch for every game, you would have a fantastic season. Most of your athletes will think this way a few times during the season, but it is difficult to get there time after time. It is particularly difficult for them to get there after something bad has happened, such as giving up a home run, taking a perfect pitch to hit, or booting the baseball, but the effort must be made. Your first task is to tell them how they should be thinking—that part is as easy as telling them the information in the preceding paragraph. Second, provide opportunities for them to practice getting into that mindset (competitive situations without your yelling to them about their mechanics) and constantly remind them of how they need to think. If you can get your athletes thinking this way on a consistent basis, you are a great coach.

PUTTING SPORT PSYCHOLOGY TO WORK FOR YOU

A great deal of information has been presented in this chapter. Hopefully, some of it sounds like something that could help you become a more effective coach if you could just incorporate it into your coaching style. The purpose of this final section is to suggest ways to do just that.

An excellent, simple way to get started helping your athletes develop their mental games is through one-on-one or small-group informal conversations. The key here is to ask a lot of questions. The two fundamental questions are (a) What were you thinking about out there? and (b) What do you want to be thinking out there? Getting them to compare their two answers can be very enlightening. Keep probing. Ask them to be more specific, and use your active listening technique.

This information can offer you invaluable insight into your players, especially when they are slumping or they are in a pressure situation. A good example is the situation described at the start of this chapter where the coach and young hitter are meeting with the game on the line. If the two of them have previously discussed what that athlete needs to do to give him the best chance of being successful at bat (how to relax and what to focus on), the coach can simply remind the player of those things. Preparing for these situations in advance helps the athlete be more confident when they arise.

Another very useful idea is to incorporate the terms and ideas presented in this chapter into your coaching lingo. Examples of this were provided in previous sections.

A third way to use the information in this chapter is to present and discuss a topic (e.g., visualization, self-talk, routines) on the field during practice the way any physical skill is introduced. Each day a different skill or concept could be talked about and a discussion generated about it. Taking time during practice, even just 10 minutes in a day, shows your players that you think the mental game is important.

One of the most important and useful ways to help your athletes work on their mental game is through the use of simulation during practice. Most successful athletes spend a great deal of their practice time trying to simulate the conditions they will actually experience in competition. Examples of this include giving a batter an important game situation during batting practice (e.g., "There are two outs, a man on third, and we're down by one"), having real base runners when you work on defensive skills (e.g., hit fungoes to the infielders, work on bunt coverages or cutoffs and relays) or making the infielders beat a certain time such as getting a ground ball to the first baseman in 4.3 seconds, and having an umpire and batter stand in during a pitcher's bull-pen workout. Another good idea for practice is to have your players occasionally practice making an error and then regrouping and focusing in on the next ball. All of these provide excellent opportunities for your athletes to practice using their mental skills in dealing with the pressures they will face on game day.

One way to motivate yourself to use the information in this chapter is to set goals for using it. Examples of good goals might be to (a) go back and actually answer the questions in the box on page 28, (b) have at least one informal sport psychology–related conversation with a player each day, or (c) present three topics in this chapter a week to your team during practice.

In conclusion, your athletes need to realize what an important role their minds play in determining their success. They need to know that, to get good results, they need to think good thoughts. Tell them to spend their time thinking about the good stuff, not dwelling on past or possible future failures. Help them, by asking them questions, to specifically identify what they need to be thinking about to give themselves the best possible chance of being successful. They will learn a lot from their own answers.

A common theme throughout this chapter has been awareness. Just as you want your athletes to be more aware of what they are thinking and doing, so that they can catch themselves when they are thinking or doing things that hinder their performance, a major purpose of this chapter was to make you more aware of some of the aspects of effective coaching. It is difficult in such a limited space to cover the many important applications sport psychology has to offer coaches. It is hoped, however, that enough information has been provided and enough questions asked to get you thinking about such things as your coaching philosophy, your abilities as a communicator and motivator, and your development of the mental game of each of your athletes.

KEYS TO SUCCESS

- Don't neglect the mental aspects of baseball in practice.
- What you do can have a big effect on your players' self-esteem.
- One of your most important jobs as coach is to create a team atmosphere conducive to successful performance.
- How effectively you can influence your team's atmosphere depends on your coaching philosophy, your communication skills, and your ability to motivate your players.
- Positive reinforcement, trusting your body, keeping control, selective perception, acting confident, visualization, self-talk, and relaxation help your athletes be as confident as possible.
- Use focusing and preperformance routines to help athletes focus on and play the game one pitch at a time.

REFERENCES AND RESOURCES

Dorfman, H.A., & Kuehl, K. (1989). *The mental game of baseball: A guide to peak performance*. South Bend, IN: Diamond Communications.

Hershiser, O. (1989). *Out of the blue*. Brentwood, TN: Wolgemuth & Hyatt.

Murray, M.C. (1986). Leadership effectiveness. In J.M. Williams (Ed.), *Applied sport psychology: Personal growth to peak performance*. Palo Alto, CA: Mayfield.

Ravizza, K. (1986). Increasing awareness for sport performance. In J.M. Williams (Ed.), *Applied sport psychology: Personal growth to peak performance* (pp. 149-162). Palo Alto, CA: Mayfield.

Ravizza, K. (1988). *Pitching, fielding, and hitting imagery tapes*. Department of Physical Education and Recreation, California State University–Fullerton, Fullerton, CA 92634.

CHAPTER 3

Biomechanics: Analyzing Skills and Performance

Lois A. Klatt
Concordia University

Your baseball season has just begun. All 18 players on the roster appear to be well conditioned and physically fit. The players seem to be strong, lean, and healthy.

Who's going to make your starting lineup? Jack drives the ball into the gaps, but Jake has a tendency to hit under the ball and pop up. Both Dave and Dan can get on base, but Dan has a tendency to score more often due to his speed. Ken and Kevin both want to play shortstop; Ken's throws are accurate while Kevin invariably puts the ball in the dirt. At first base, Bob has trouble with throws in the dirt, while Bill is able to pick them up. Why is Steve always ready to play, whereas Scott always seems to have a bad shoulder or elbow or ankle?

Maximal performance with minimal injury is possible for your players only with proper mechanics. As a coach you can help your players turn outs into hits and singles into doubles and strive toward errorless baseball. You also can give your players appropriate baseball conditioning to prevent injury. By increasing your knowledge and understanding of biomechanical principles in general, you can begin to apply them to achieve proper baseball mechanics for improved performance on the field with fewer injuries.

WHY BIOMECHANICS IS IMPORTANT

From the pros to Little League, baseball is a game of seconds, inches, and power. What is the fastest, most effective way to steal second base? How do you pitch with velocity and control? How do you hit a ball out of the park? Coaches and players are challenged by such *how* and *what* questions; answers form the foundation for successful baseball.

Baseball demands maximum proficiency in a variety of skills such as batting, running, catching, and throwing. Other sports are based on only one or two similar sport skills; for example, tennis uses a forehand and backhand drive to play both offense and defense. Effective practices, sport-related fitness, and biomechanical principles demand the attention of today's coach.

Because practice makes permanent, and only perfect practice makes perfect, players must practice proper skill mechanics over and over again to permanently learn the correct skill movement or pattern. To become efficient at their skills, athletes need effective conditioning programs that are both progressive and specific to their sports.

Biomechanics is the study of applied anatomy and mechanical laws of motion that effect human performance. Through biomechanics you can better understand how the human body moves, and you can become more knowledgeable about effective and efficient movement patterns that maximize performance and minimize injury.

To help your baseball players perform more effectively and efficiently, you need to understand the ultimate purpose of each baseball skill. The primary purpose usually is expressed in mechanical terms such as force and accuracy. To hit behind the runner going from first to second requires accuracy; this objective is primary—if the ball is not accurately placed, the hit may result in a double play. To hit a line drive out of the ball park, the ultimate objective is maximum distance (speed or horizontal force).

The more skilled baseball player is able to satisfy a greater number of physical demands in his performance. He has a greater range of movement from the trunk to the extremities, and dynamic balance takes on a new dimension. Physical laws of motion must be applied to change direction rapidly, time the release point, hit the ball with the "sweet spot" of the bat, maximize velocity, and perform skill patterns at one's highest level of baseball competition.

Baseball players have a tendency to add their own batting, running, and throwing styles or individual idiosyncrasies to skills. To be a successful coach, you need to learn how to analyze skills and apply this knowledge to each player's performance, including eliminating individual style quirks that limit performance. You have a responsibility to teach players how to arrive at the desired outcome: to maximize force with control and accuracy while preventing injury. If you coach in this way, your players will be able to participate to their fullest and to enjoy the game of baseball for a long time.

BIOMECHANICAL CONCERNS IN BASEBALL

Biomechanics is a science of action. It examines the effect of internal forces (muscles) and external forces (gravity, air resistance) on human movement and skilled performance. Biomechanical analysis has become indispensable in the coaching profession.

General laws of mechanics offer a sound, logical basis for analyzing and evaluating essential and efficient movement patterns in baseball. A biomechanical approach is necessary to determine offensive and defensive skill patterns, new trends, and individual performance. A successful coach is able to determine the basis for a developmental process and put new ideas, rather than individual idiosyncrasies, into practice.

Biomechanical principles and concepts will help you understand balance and stability, forces of opposition, trunk and neuromuscular systems, and other related principles.

How Do Balance and Stability Affect Performance?

The more skilled a player becomes, the greater is his dynamic or moving balance. Dynamic balance is seen as a player leaps into the air to catch a high line-drive under controlled speed and direction; a sense of equilibrium and harmony come to mind as you observe skilled performance.

Stability means the ability to resist forces, both internal and external. Joint stability involves equal amounts of muscular strength over a joint (e.g., front/back and inside/outside of the thigh). The joint thus is able to withstand motion and absorb shock without injury and to resist outside forces such as gravity that would affect the total body's equilibrium.

Proficiency in throwing, batting, running, and fielding skills progresses from the ground up or from the "grass roots." A balanced base of support is essential before, during, and after the skill is performed, for maximum effect and efficiency of movement. A loss of balance during *any* part of a skill sequence diminishes the speed of the bat or thrown ball and alters the skill pattern.

The base of support should be the entire foot area that is in contact with the ground with the line of gravity in front of the ankle bone. "Get up on your toes, weight forward" is something many coaches tell their players, but the ball of the foot provides a much smaller base of support than the entire foot.

The *ready position* in baseball is essential to both defense (as in fielding) and offense (as in preparing to steal a base). The most effective ready position begins from the ground up with a full-foot, shoulder-width stance. Hips, knees, and ankles are comfortably bent. The trunk is extended, with the player's head over and in line with the base of support. The arms are held comfortably away from the trunk, free to move, with elbows bent approximately 90 to 120 degrees (Figure 3.1). This ready position results in the fastest movement and reaction time in all directions—forward/backward, side-to-side, and rotary.

Figure 3.1 Ready position.

A balanced player is *centered* when his movement and concentration are focused on his center of gravity (mid pelvis area), the point of equilibrium. To test a player's balance in the ready position, ask him to take the ready position and concentrate on his center of gravity or centering point. Then push him in a surprise direction (forward, sideward, rotary). If the player remains stable, he is centered and ready.

Why Does the Coach Need to Consider the Mechanics of Opposite Forces?

As you observe external movement and study internal skill patterns, keep in mind the following three major principles of opposite forces: (a) equal and opposite reaction, (b) acceleration and deceleration, and (c) centripetal and centrifugal force.

Every coach must keep in mind that when a player pushes down against a playing surface, the ground, base, or pitching rubber pushes back. "For every action there is an equal and opposite reaction." The harder a player drives his legs into the ground, the harder the ground pushes back. When a player drives his foot down and back, he will move up and forward.

All forces in the human body work on the same equal-and-opposite-reaction principle. The source of force in the human body is muscle action. Before a muscle shortens, it lengthens; contraction that shortens the muscle is termed *concentric;* contraction that lengthens a muscle is called *eccentric.* Here are some common baseball examples of such movements: (a) The front or anterior muscles over the throwing shoulder joint lengthen eccentrically as the arm drives back, before shortening as the arm throws forward. (b) When a player runs, his calf muscle lengthens over the ankle and heel bone as the foot drives down and back, before contracting concentrically on the ground pushoff. (c) Before a player hits the baseball during a swing, the posterior muscles over the front or lead shoulder lengthen (contract eccentrically) before shortening as the bat is pulled around.

Factors of opposition are also related to direction changes. On an extra-base hit the runner changes his path or direction to first base by driving the right foot down and right into the ground to round first base and go on to second.

Another pair of opposites in mechanical movement is acceleration (speeding up) and deceleration (slowing down). Whatever the desired direction, one set of muscles produces (accelerates) that movement and the body's opposite set of muscles reduces (decelerates) the movement. In throwing, the anterior muscles at the shoulder joint initiate forward movement, and the posterior muscles over the back of the shoulder joint are used to slow down, or decelerate, the upper extremity (Figure 3.2).

Prime-mover muscles are referred to as *agonists,* and their opposing muscles are termed *antagonists.* Conditioning programs need to consider the antagonist muscles as well as the prime-mover muscles.

Consider "crack the whip" or skaters skating around in a circle linked together. The center person (axis) pulls in, and the end person wants to fly off on a tangent. The same thing occurs in baseball. Whether a defensive player is throwing sidearm or overhand, a whiplike pattern is

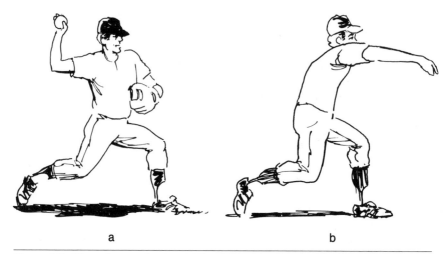

a   b

Figure 3.2 Throwing mechanics. (a) Front shoulder muscles accelerate the arm (ball). (b) Back or posterior shoulder muscles decelerate the arm.

performed. Skilled movement patterns use the body and its extremities as a whip. The shoulder joint is an excellent example. Muscles over the shoulder joint must contract and maintain the joint's stability on a throw to counteract the dislocating force of momentum generated during a throw. To prevent or minimize injuries in baseball, your conditioning program must address both centrifugal and centripetal forces. Centrifugal forces pull out and want to dislocate; centripetal forces pull in.

The reaction of the ball opposite to the ground or bat also needs to be considered. If both the ground and the ball are resilient (and usually they are), the ball comes off the ground at the same angle at which it arrived. Some fields "give" more than others on ground contact, reducing the speed of the ball and causing it to rebound at a lower angle. When the ball contacts the ground, it develops a ground friction that causes the top of the ball to spin faster, lowering its rebound angle relative to the ground. If a ball hits the ground while spinning backward, a higher bounce results (Figure 3.3).

The bat–ball reaction also involves opposites. For the most effective bat–ball contact, the ball needs to be hit through its center of gravity; if it is not, force is lost in added ball spin. If the bat makes even contact with the ball, the ball's direction is influenced upward if contacted below the center of gravity, and downward if contacted above the center of gravity. A high fly ball in baseball is due to the batter overstriding, lowering the body's center of gravity and bat level, and hitting under the ball.

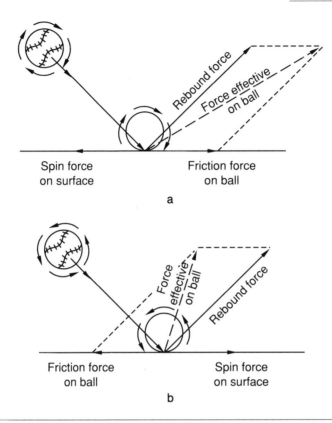

Figure 3.3   Field reaction and the effect of spin. (a) Topspin. (b) Backspin.

What Are the Mechanical Components of Efficient Skill Performance?

In addition to observing the whole player, a coach must view the body parts as separate segments. Each segment is linked to another; all segments need to be practiced sequentially in as gamelike a manner as possible. All throwing and batting skills begin from the ground up, or from the base segment—the most stable part of the system, the lower extremities. As the forward stride is taken and a stable ground support is maintained, forward hip rotation is initiated, which begins the sequence of joint action from the midline (proximal) to the upper extremity or distal segment. Sequentially the trunk then rotates forward, followed by the shoulder, elbow, and wrist.

Each body segment must come forward as the preceding movement or proximal segment reaches its greatest speed (angular velocity), to develop maximum force in throwing or batting (e.g., hips–trunk–shoulder–elbow–wrist). A sequential pattern includes a "lagging back" of the distal body part (arm) as the more proximal segments (hips and trunk) are accelerated forward (Figure 3.4).

Figure 3.4   "Lagging back" action of the throwing arm; the final positioning of the hand prior to release due to effective sequential throwing mechanics.

Should a Coach Emphasize Accuracy or Force?

Accuracy is critically important in the sport of baseball, but sport skill patterns are determined by the sequence and speed of joint (muscle) action or force. Start early to develop mechanically correct force patterns so there is time to develop a *controlled* force pattern. Many players are working on knuckleballs and split-finger average fastballs instead of reaching back and force throwing. Off-speed pitchers have a tendency to concentrate too much on the arm motion and reduce the forward hip rotation that is essential in throwing.

Accuracy is nothing more than a slight direction modification at time of release: a little early or late, a little to the right or left. In many cases, stability and balance corrections eliminate a player's accuracy problem. Accuracy can also be enhanced with the forward stride. A forward stride flattens the path of the hand, ball, or the bat and allows the player a greater amount of time and distance for accuracy.

Movement is efficient when a minimum amount of force or energy is utilized with maximum results. Top baseball players perform ballistically:

muscle force is used to initiate the skill action, and then relaxation takes over. When a sequential skill pattern is initiated from the ground up, utilizing a forward stride that drives the hips or pelvis into the action, the upper extremity moves with momentum and a minimum amount of muscular force.

What Contributes to Peak Skill Performance?

Biomechanically, the neuromuscular and skeletal systems have strong implications for conditioning movement patterns and minimizing injuries. Neuromuscular aspects include force–velocity, stretch–reflex, and coil–recoil relationships.

Baseball utilizes considerable muscle power. Lower extremity power is needed for running. Batting and throwing are examples of skills involving upper extremity muscular power. Power equals muscle strength times joint speed. Baseball skill patterns place a high premium on speed of contraction as compared to muscle strength or muscle endurance.

Muscles also contain an elastic stretch reflex that, when used, increases tension and produces maximum muscle force. Biomechanists look at this as elastic or energy storage. Upper extremity (shoulder, elbow, wrist) and lower extremity (hip, knee, ankle) conditioning programs need to include this prestretch with speed for maximum force and power. The faster the prestretch, the greater the power; this is the concept behind plyometrics.

Explosive power essential in hitting and throwing is produced by a coiling or tight-spring effect used to initiate a skill. For example, in the

Figure 3.5   "Coiling" effect produced by the back leg during the preparation phase in batting (also throwing).

preliminary position for throwing and batting, the back hip, knee, ankle, and trunk start coiled as in a cocked gun (Figure 3.5). This coiling effect results in energy storage by the muscles.

The body has many neuromuscular reflexes, such as tonic neck, inner ear, and righting reflexes. These reflexes contribute to purposeful movement. The body follows and adjusts its position relative to head movement. If the head is thrown back over the right shoulder, stepping back with the right foot is more efficient. Keeping a steady head and tracking the ball with the eyes stabilizes a batter. Joints and surrounding tissues contain special sensory receptors that give rise to the kinesthetic or body sense: how the body knows it feels right. Performance qualities are improved when such reflexes and specialized senses are integrated into training and conditioning programs.

What Mechanical Factors Influence the Flight of a Baseball?

Where a batted or thrown baseball ends up depends on many mechanical principles. Gravity always pulls the ball down at 32 feet per second per second (9.8 meters per second per second). "Whatever goes up will come down." The greater the speed of the baseball, the greater the air resistance, which always moves exactly opposite to the direction the ball is traveling, causing it to change direction. A spinning baseball always moves away from the spin, because pressure builds up on the spinning surface area. One of the fun aspects about a knuckle- or nonspinning ball is that it has no fixed direction; it is completely at the mercy of the irregular air pressure around it. How long a baseball remains in the air is determined by its speed and angle of projection. The higher the angle, the greater the *hang* time or the time the ball remains in the air.

What Should the Coach Know About Consistent Throwing?

Your number one pitcher returns from semester break with a sore shoulder. Did he throw too much? Too hard? He says he followed his practice outline and didn't overdo anything; it just happened. Is this a problem for the trainer? The team doctor? No, the first diagnosis should come from the coach. As you analyze your player's pitching form, you discover that his hips are late in driving forward and around. This reduces the effectiveness of the body's largest and most powerful force producers, the legs and hips. Because of the mechanical error, the pitching shoulder was working much harder than necessary. This acute shoulder pain is the first sign of improper technique, which leads to most chronic shoulder injuries common in baseball.

What Are the Mechanics of an Ideal Throw?

The preparation phase initiates body motion, individual timing, and rhythm, and places the thrower into the most efficient and effective position for maximum force and control.

The throwing action is initiated by swinging both hands upward toward the chest and extending the throwing arm downward, backward, and upward to shoulder level, accompanied by a 90-degree foot, hip, and upper body pivot. The striding leg, knee bent, moves toward the body as the trunk is inclined backward over the support leg. The back leg is slightly bent at the hip, knee, and ankle; a coiling or spring effect takes place on the inside of the back leg and hip in preparation for driving forward into the throw.

The force phase involves the forward forces generated by the entire body and whiplike action of the arm; it includes a split second of the time following the ball's release to ensure that the ball leaves the hand with maximum velocity.

Body momentum and throwing rhythm continue in a forward direction by swinging the striding leg forward (bent at the knee) and the nonthrowing arm across the body and back with a bent elbow. The shoulder of the throwing arm is outwardly (laterally) rotated, and the elbow is bent to an approximate 90-degree position to facilitate the arm's extreme range of movement. The back leg is vigorously extended or uncoiled, driving the throw forward into the stride position.

All of these movements serve to increase the distance through which the thrower can apply force to the ball, increasing the energy and magnitude of velocity imparted to the ball.

The striding leg of a pitcher lands just beyond an imaginary line running from the middle of the pitching rubber to the middle of home plate. The hip, knee, and ankle are in a slightly bent position. When the striding foot contacts the ground, the hips and trunk accelerate and rotate forward as the upper arm outwardly rotates maximally, bringing the elbow forward and upward, leaving the throwing forearm and hand well behind. The trunk leans away from the throwing arm; the shoulder maintains its horizontal position as the elbow repositions itself into extension at 110 to 160 degrees. Then the forearm is whipped forward sequentially, and the ball is released in the direction of the target (Figure 3.6). The efficiency of throwing comes from the fact that a minimum amount of muscle force is used by the shoulder, elbow, and wrist to produce the desired movement, because the movement is ballistic.

A complete follow-through includes a balanced stride-leg position, trunk flexion, and the throwing arm positioned across the body and

Figure 3.6   A skilled overhand throw. Note the lateral body lean to accommodate elbow extension.

angled downward toward the stride foot. The weight shifts slightly forward, with the pivot leg and foot coming into a ready position. This phase guarantees time for the antagonistic muscles to slow down the fast-moving throwing arm and not cut short the production of maximum ball speed.

What Throwing Issues Do Coaches Challenge?

There are several biomechanical questions that coaches frequently ask about throwing.

- Is there an optimum stride length? The increase in stride length should be a gradual process, with change occurring only as the player is able to maintain stability. The average thrower has a stride length approximately 50% of his body height. According to research, a suggested guideline for optimal stride length is 80% to 90% of body height for pitching at 80 miles or more per hour.
- Does stride length vary with type of pitch or windup? According to the literature, stride length is consistent regardless of windup, set stance, or type of pitch being thrown (Atwater, 1977).
- Does windup or set stance affect ball speed? Speed, or velocity at time of release, has little relationship to windup or set stance. The need for and effectiveness of a windup needs to be reexamined (Atwater, 1977).
- What is the angle between the thrower's forearm and the horizontal position as viewed from the front or rear at time of release? The

angle increases from 100 to 170 degrees as skill and ball velocity increases.

- Is the ball-release height level with or slightly above the head? It varies with the individual thrower's technique. As the thrower leans away from the throwing side, the height of release only appears to be higher; the arm's action remains the same. Leaning laterally allows greater range of motion; this increase in lean occurs progressively as the player becomes better able to maintain stability.

Sidearm throwing and overarm throwing consist of similar movement patterns. In sidearm throwing, the body's lean is toward the throwing side (quick), and in throwing overarm (farther), the body leans away from the throwing side (Atwater, 1977) (see Figure 3.7).

Figure 3.7   Baseball sidearm and overarm throwing. Note the similar arm patterns with opposite direction of body lean.

What Should the Coach Know About Aggressive Hitting?

A new recruit comes to your team with great batting potential. His swing is smooth and powerful. However, he has a tendency to strike out. Where do you start? Does he need more batting practice? A different bat? Maybe. But if he has a mechanical error, neither of these solutions will eliminate the problem. Knowing good batting mechanics, you start the analysis from the ground up. Perhaps after determining a reference point, you observe that his stride length is inconsistent; it changes with each pitch, and in most instances it is too long. By overstriding, the batter causes the center of gravity of his body and of the bat to fall below the height of the pitched ball.

To Have a Chance at .300 or Better, What Mechanics Should Your Hitter Demonstrate?

In the preparation/stance phase, response time to the pitch, actual movement time, and bat velocity are critical; the batter must be ready mentally and physically. The initial stance begins from the ground up with a minimum amount of tension.

The hips and shoulders are parallel with the pitch's line of flight, with the rear foot positioned approximately 90 degrees to the line of flight. The hips and the knee and ankle of the back leg are slightly bent. The feet are about shoulder-width apart with body weight concentrated over the rear foot.

The bat should be gripped with the fingers rather than held deep in the palms of the hands; this grip releases tension in the forearms and wrists. The bat is then brought back and pointed upward; a position midway between horizontal and vertical provides an average bat resistance. Hands should be located at the top of the back shoulder. The back elbow is held slightly away from the body, and the front arm and elbow are raised to the top of the strike zone.

The most important aspect of the preparation phase preceding forward motion is the coiling or spring effect developed on the inside of the leg and hip to prepare for the driving force forward into the swing. This coiling sensation should be felt in the inside of the back leg, up through the trunk, and to the back of the forward shoulder.

In the force/swing phase, the batter initiates forward movement by lifting the front foot just off the ground, shifting the body weight forward, and driving the back leg vigorously into the ground. The stride should be 6 to 10 inches in length, and the stride foot should land in the *same* location for every pitch, regardless of whether the pitch is high or low, inside or outside. The stride leg is slightly bent as ground contact is made, and balance is maintained throughout the entire swing. Every effort should be made to maintain ground contact with the rear foot for maximum power and stability. The front leg produces a counterforce that causes the pelvis to rotate forward, followed by trunk rotation. The upper body is then brought forward horizontally, being led by the back of the front shoulder. The forward elbow straightens immediately (almost straight) to increase the length of the lever and develop maximum velocity (Figure 3.8). At the same time, the back arm continues to "throw" from the inside out to accommodate the level or horizontal swing. Rapid acceleration of the straight front arm leaves the hands and bat well behind. The hands and bat then whip forward, and bat–ball contact is made as the arms roll over and wrists snap through on the follow-through.

Figure 3.8 Good batting mechanics begin from the ground up: a balanced and consistent stride, pelvic rotation, followed by trunk rotation and an extended front elbow.

Muscle forces only contribute to hip and trunk rotation and the initiation of shoulder rotation. Due to the summation of forces and centrifugal force, the arms and wrists are moving at such speeds (100 miles per hour) that muscles cannot catch up to their velocities. Thus upper body movements are initiated muscularly and completed ballistically, through muscle relaxation.

The head should remain stationary or adjust slightly to differentiate among "moving" pitches. The chin is tucked down into the forward shoulder. Eye tracking is essential, with a minimum amount of head movement; be sure your players are able to see the ball over the plate, both inside and outside. (Eyes are able to see the ball within 3 to 5 inches of the plate.)

The follow-through is responsible for the production of maximum force and continuity of the whiplike sequential action. Factors to look for during the follow-through include a balanced body position from the ground up, square pelvis (belt buckle facing the pitcher), upper body movement in the direction of ball flight, and arm and wrist roll after ball contact.

What Hitting Issues Do Coaches Challenge?

The following are questions that coaches frequently ask about hitting.

- Should the batter stand in the back or front or toward the inside or outside of the box? Location in the batter's box depends on batting reaction time and the bat's movement time, as well as on the pitcher's ability to throw with speed and breaking action. The back position gives the batter more time to swing at a faster ball and more time to determine whether the off-speed breaking pitch is in the strike zone. Standing in the front of the box leaves less time for the ball to break away from the plate. Location is also affected by the size (reach) of the batter in relation to the width of the box. The proper side-to-side position depends entirely on the batter's ability to cover the entire plate area with the "sweet" part of the bat.

- Should the batter use an open or closed stance? A forward and backward or square stance is assumed in the batter's box by most hitters. An open stance, with the hips and shoulders rotated to face the pitcher, allows the hitter to get the bat around faster because it has to travel a shorter distance due to its shorter backswing. Hitters who are able to bring the bat around faster can use a closed stance, with hips and shoulders facing slightly away from the pitcher. This position provides a longer swing time for imparting greater distance, due to a greater preparation phase and greater force to the ball.

- Is the best initial bat position midway between horizontal and vertical? A low horizontal position provides the least bat resistance, and a straight-up or perpendicular position provides the greatest bat resistance.

- What bat length is appropriate? Bat length is important because the shorter the bat (including a choke grip), the faster the movement. A longer bat has greater resistance, but the end of the bat travels farther, producing more power. If the batter can move a longer bat around quickly, this would be the best choice.

- Does the type of bat make a difference? The greater the bat's stiffness or resilience, the greater its rebounding properties—and the farther the ball will go. One of the reasons the metal bat is not used in professional baseball is its greater resilience compared to a wooden bat.

- How is speed incorporated into conditioning? Skill patterns need to be practiced as they will be performed in competition. Plyometrics and use of rubber medicine balls are effective in developing hip and trunk rotation and initiating upper body action, thus contributing to bat speed.

- How is maximum power developed? The batter produces maximum bat speed from the ground up; the stride forward is followed by hip and trunk rotation and finally the upper extremities. A common error in batting is to pull the handle too early during the forward stride (an "arm" swing); this eliminates the summation of forces and sequential action.

- What stride length is appropriate? A short stride compared to a longer stride reduces the lowering of the center of gravity and maintains a good head position. The principal advantages of a short stride seem to be that (a) the batter's center of gravity remains close to the back foot and allows for a faster, more forceful hip rotation during the swing, and (b) the smaller range of motion leaves less chance for error and thus improves the batter's chance of obtaining consistency (Hay, 1985).

- Is batting off a batting tee helpful? If batting tees are used, practice correct head positioning and eye tracking during each swing from a specific reference point so the pattern isn't changed. The reference point may be a stationary marker 60 feet away or, in limited space, a closer reference point that still requires a change in focus.
- Can a batter's reaction time be improved? Research indicates that top players have faster reactions and swing times than below-.300, average hitters, who have longer decision times. Coaches need to work on reaction time, which includes swing time (Breen, 1967). Concentrated practice with full swings using visual, rapid cues (colored or marked balls, lights, etc.) improves reaction time.
- When does a batter actually swing? The batter coils the bat backward at the time the pitch is released; the batter begins to swing when the ball is halfway to the plate (Breen, 1967).

What Is Proper Bunting Technique?

Bunting, a great offensive weapon, utilizes many biomechanical principles. A stable base of support, forward and backward in the direction of the line of force, aids dynamic balance. The purpose of the bunt needs careful consideration. Is a sacrifice bunt desired, or do you want a bunt single? The desired distance and direction from home plate determines whether the bunter produces or reduces the ball's force by "catching" it on the end of the bat. Know how and where you want your player to put the ball. For maximum control, the top or barrel hand controls the production or reduction of force, and direction is determined by the handle or bottom hand (Figure 3.9). Since every bunt should be directed down, the bat should be held at the top of the strike zone to be sure the ball is contacted above its center of gravity and is deflected downward.

Figure 3.9   Skilled bunting.

What Should the Coach Know About Fielding?

Your center fielder starts to move in on a fly ball hit over his head! Why? Applying biomechanical principles of balance and force as you analyze each player's actions, it becomes evident that your player is not in a proper ready position, able to move in any direction. Your player was ready to move in only one direction, forward.

A fielder needs to be in a position that allows movement in any direction. If two or three steps are taken in place before moving, it may be too late. To test your fielders for ready position, toss or throw balls in every direction in front of and beyond them, and watch their immediate ground reactions and footwork as they move for the balls. You are looking for a shift in body weight and a pivot move in the direction of the toss.

Every fielder should be encouraged to get behind the ball and into a throwing position before the ball arrives. If the fielder throws right-handed, the ball should be fielded on the right side with the right foot back. Too often the fielder runs unnecessarily and is taken away from the throw by momentum. Both hands should be used for every catch within normal reach; only stretch catches should be executed with just the glove hand. Most habitual one-handers are unable to execute an effective catch-and-throw when needed.

In catching, the objective is to gradually reduce the ball's forces by using distance and time. Each body part sequentially gives to reduce forces. Today's gloves are very effective in reducing ball spin and providing a large surface area to reduce the ball's force.

What Mechanics Need to Be Considered in Catching?

When a player is preparing to receive an oncoming ball, his feet should be separated slightly in a forward/backward stride to enlarge his base of support in the direction of the forces that must be resisted to provide stability. Every effort should be made to bring the body in line with the approaching ball so that the forces can be received close to the body's center of gravity. As the ball hits the glove, the hands are pulled in toward the body, and the body's weight is transferred to the back foot to increase the distance over which the forces can be reduced (Figure 3.10). When the catch is to be followed by a throw, the momentum of the oncoming ball should be transferred toward the side of the throwing arm; the give becomes the backswing or preparation phase of the throw that follows.

The position of the hands in catching is the single most important factor in avoiding injuries. The hands should be positioned with fingers pointing upward when the ball is received above waist height and pointing downward when catching below the waist.

If the ball is caught away from the throwing side, the leg on the catching side is back on the catch and used as a pivot. The fielder continues moving

Figure 3.10 Effective positioning in fielding a ground ball.

and transfers momentum into the throw by taking another step back and around and into the throw.

Movement time to the ball is fastest when the head moves in the direction of the ball. For example, if a ball is hit up and over either shoulder, the pivot and running movement is fastest when the head is moved up and back. The head initiates a directional change, in that it places the body's center of gravity in that line of movement.

What Should the Coach Know About Effective Baserunning?

Your batter hits a ground ball deep in the hole and is thrown out. Is your player just slow? As you become aware of the problem, you notice that the runner has good speed once started but is not able to get out of the batter's box quickly. Through continued observation and concentrated analysis you become aware of your batter's lack of balance and extra foot adjustment on the swing and follow-through.

The best defense in the world is not going to win games. To win, at some point in the game at least one offensive player must run the bases and reach home successfully. Taking first things first, the batter must become a base runner. Studies have shown that right-handed hitters are able to get out of the batter's box slightly faster than left-handed batters. A left-handed batter, on the other hand, is closer to first base by three or four feet. The left-hander, based on time and distance, can reach first 0.2 to 0.3 seconds faster than a right-handed batter. Because baseball is a game of seconds and inches, becoming a batter–base runner needs to be practiced. Film and video analysis show that at bat–ball contact, the back foot just clears the ground and the batter's weight is stabilized on the front foot. Dynamic balance at this time is essential for effectively becoming a base runner. The body's weight is shifted back onto the rear foot, and then the first step is initiated somewhat forward toward first base.

Becoming a batter–base runner depends on quickness and not necessarily on speed. With a consistent stride and weight shift in batting and a reduction of forces following a complete swing, developed through directed practice, the batter can become an effective base runner.

What's the Best Method of Rounding a Base?

Baserunning on any extra-base hit employs the technique of changing direction to round a base and head for the next. The shortest distance between bases is a straight line; however, this would include a 90-degree left turn, forcing the runner to almost come to a stop.

Most methods generally used to round a base and go on to the next are effective. Rounding the bases is an individual performance based on success and time. Each player needs to determine an appropriate personal technique through tests timed on running and rounding the bases. Time a 60-foot straight-out run, or have the player hit off a tee and run to first or to second. Running straight as long as possible and then maintaining momentum as a change in direction takes place is the goal. Due to centrifugal force the body wants to fly off into the outfield or at a tangent; the outside foot must push the center of gravity back inside. Tagging the base with the inside foot allows the runner to establish effective foot-to-ground contact with the outside, or right, foot producing the greatest amount of friction between the ground and the spikes.

What's the Most Effective Means of Tagging Up on a Fly Ball?

Time studies tell us that a moving start results in the fastest takeoff. Many coaches use a verbal or visual cue for the tag-up. To put movement into the body, one foot is placed comfortably on the front edge of the base and the other leg is placed on the ground behind the base. A signal starts the runner's movement a split second before the catch. The back foot moves out first; thus base contact is maintained until the ball is caught. Timing is critical, but the moving start can be used most effectively. Once again, practicing this technique can take the needed time off the run and possibly score the winning run.

What's the Best Technique for Stealing a Base?

Stealing a base is one of the offensive joys, a close second to hitting successfully. A walking lead-off from first base, which keeps momentum in the body, has proven to be the most successful means, compared to a stationary lead. Good pitchers, however, should be able to make a base runner stop before the ball is pitched.

What is the most effective set position for stealing second base without being picked off first? The base runner leaves first base in a side stride position with about three and a half shuffle (not crossover) steps (12 to

15 feet) from the base. To establish a good base of support, the entire foot should be on the ground, with feet positioned shoulder-width apart or slightly wider (according to individual preference). To ensure maximum reaction time toward second base or back to first, the center of gravity must be centered. When the signal to steal is received, the body's weight is shifted toward the right leg as the left leg pushes into the ground. The right arm, with elbow bent, drives backward for an equal and opposite reaction. A somewhat upright trunk position provides the axis for rotation. The drive onto the pivot foot is immediate, followed by an explosive drive down the base path with the left leg and right arm (Fig. 3.11). Centering when in the set position is most important for directional change.

c   b   a

Figure 3.11   Stealing second. (a) Start in the ready position. (b) Shift weight onto the right foot, pivot, and drive the right elbow back. (c) Immediately drive down and back with the right leg and left arm.

To come to a stop at second base, the runner must redirect momentum. If the runner remains standing, he must lean the center of gravity backward and overstride the last two or three steps to redirect the forces. If he slides, ground friction will provide the retarding force needed to overcome the body's momentum. The objective is to provide a minimum loss of forward speed. Sliding head-first may reduce total time by 0.1 seconds, but the vulnerability of the position may not merit it. The time for change in direction has been shown to be the same for the foot-first slide as for the stand-up position; the need to avoid a tag would determine your choice of arrival technique.

What Mechanics Need to Be Considered in Sliding?

To slide, a runner must move from a sprinting position to a near-horizontal position without undue loss of speed by rotating forward 70 to 85 degrees into a head-first slide or backward 70 to 95 degrees into a feet-first slide. The bent-leg slide is the safest slide to execute, because the forces of impact are distributed over a larger surface area and the spikes are less likely to be caught in the ground. Continuity between the run at full speed and the takeoff requires that there be no leap or jump. Sliding too early increases friction and slows down speed for a longer period of time; sliding too late increases the chance of injury, as the slider's body hits the bag with greater force.

The runner runs into the slide and leans back when about 8 to 10 feet from the base. The striding foot (whichever one is most natural) extends slightly upward and forward toward the bag. As the center of gravity shifts backward behind the base of support, the runner pushes off the support (takeoff) leg and bends it approximately 90 degrees, tucking it up under the knee of the extended forward leg. The arms are held high and out to the side for balance. At this point, the top leg is slightly bent, with the kneecap facing up; the foot is slightly off the ground with the toes pointing up so the spikes cannot catch. The head is slightly forward, eyes focused on the base. The body is turned slightly to the side of the bent leg. The force of impact, as the body comes to the ground, is absorbed primarily by the thigh part of the bottom leg, followed by the buttocks (gluteals) and back (Figure 3.12).

Figure 3.12   Bent-leg sliding mechanics (the safest slide).

PUTTING BIOMECHANICS TO WORK FOR YOU

The coach must start with himself: the "how" to develop an analytic eye. Now the coach is ready to help the players analyze their skills. Knowing when, where, and how to use video to assess baseball skills will help you and your players toward a winning baseball season with a minimum amount of injury.

How Can the Coach Develop an Analytic Eye?

Through many years of practice and trial and error the trained coach learns to recognize effective, efficient, and skilled performance. Some errors may be identified by experienced coaches after only a few general observations. However, both novice and veteran coaches can benefit from the following suggested principles (Adrian & Cooper, 1989):

1. Because movement and forces begin from the ground up, observe the base of support throughout the skill to determine stability and direction of force.
2. View the direction of the body's weight from start to finish through the center of gravity. The center of gravity is usually within the pelvis, which in combination with the trunk is the largest and slowest-moving part of the body. It is the axis of rotation around which the extremities move.
3. The head position is important because the body follows the head due to neck and balance (inner ear and visual) reflexes. Look for head stability.
4. View a player's skill many times to determine a general feel for the performance and to assess all the separate body parts in motion.
5. Observe the performer from a variety of location points. The most effective vantage point is perpendicular or at a 90-degree angle to the major direction of movement (e.g., side, rear).
6. Determine an effective distance between the player and yourself that allows you to observe all parts of his body and the complete skill from beginning to end. Determine one or two reference points in the background (a vertical fence post, a horizontal bleacher plank) to aid in assessing body and body-part displacement.
7. We all have our biases; the power of human concentration is such that we see what we expect or want to see. Look for unusual clues in order to eliminate these biases and make an effective analysis.
8. Skill patterns are sequential; each action relates to the previous action. Observe the pattern from beginning to end, including the direction of the follow-through; conversely, trace the total motion from the termination point back to its inception.
9. Determine a visual or mental model of the skill being performed and compare the live action to the model. Models need to be like the individuals you're comparing them with; children need to be compared with children of similar skills and size, and a 6-foot slender

male with long arms and legs must be compared to a subject with similar characteristics.

10. Because movement skills are so fast and difficult for the human eye to see, view movies and videos of the particular skill at regular speed and in slow motion; in this way, you'll be able to identify more effectively the specific movements.

How Can the Coach Help a Player Analyze Performance?

You need to work with each individual player. A great variety of teaching aids are available, and the greater the number of senses that can be used in the learning process, the better the player's understanding—and with practice, a change in technique can result.

Most players are visual learners: "Show me" is the request. Our ears can be trained to differentiate good and bad performance through time intervals between sounds, and force is perceived through a change in loudness. Encourage the development of a player's kinesthetic sense, his body's feeling of motion. "Can you feel the difference?" "What does it feel like?" These questions, asked immediately after the desired movement has occurred, can help players focus on feeling the correction. A word of caution: Frequently the desired change in a pattern, although performed correctly, will feel wrong because it is new or different to the player. Have the player focus on the new feeling first; as the correction becomes automatic, it can be identified as feeling right.

As you communicate with your player(s), convey no more than two or three facts at a time. Break down all skill information into no more than three important points or component parts at a time. The more critical the correction, the fewer cues you should present at one time.

When you critique a player's skill, form a visual picture of correct skill performance. Look at the three main body parts: lower extremities, trunk and head, and upper extremities. Review the specific-skill mechanic sheets in Tables 3.1, 3.2, 3.3, and 3.4 (throwing, fielding, batting, running) and determine one cue for each body part. Develop a mental picture of the specific skill during each phase—the preparation, force, and follow-through. For example, for the follow-through phase: stable front *leg*, slightly bent; *trunk* bent and rotated away from the throwing side; and *arm* down across the body toward the ground.

To reinforce the visual cues and develop a better understanding of skill patterns, work one-on-one so that each athlete can experience and develop the pattern kinesthetically.

You may have to assist or resist the player as he initiates his throwing pattern. Have the player move through his throwing pattern while you

Table 3.1
Throwing Mechanics Analysis

Mechanics (progressive)	Rating	Comments
Preparation phase:		
Relaxed standing position	_____	_____
Pitching arm extended down and back	_____	_____
Weight on bent back leg (hip, knee, ankle)	_____	_____
Front leg up and bent at knee	_____	_____
Trunk lean back on pivot foot	_____	_____
Pivot foot, hips, and shoulders 90 degree to flight line	_____	_____
Back leg and hip coiled on inside	_____	_____
Force phase, release:		
Weight shift forward	_____	_____
Stride leg swings forward (knee bent)	_____	_____
Nonpitching arm swings back and across body (elbow bent)	_____	_____
Shoulders outward (lateral) rotation	_____	_____
Shoulder/humerus at 90-degree angle to trunk	_____	_____
Back hip and leg drive body forward, inwardly rotate, extend	_____	_____
Stride forward, counterforce maintained	_____	_____
Consistent stride length and direction (left of flight line)	_____	_____
Trunk rotation, flexion, lateral flexion	_____	_____
Shoulder outward to inward rotation, elbow lead	_____	_____
Trunk leans away from throwing arm	_____	_____
Elbow extension, 110- to 160- degree angle maintained	_____	_____
Release of ball slightly above head	_____	_____

(Cont.)

Table 3.1
(Continued)

Mechanics (progressive)	Rating	Comments
Follow-through phase:		
Balance after ball release, front leg planted	_____	_____
Direction of arm: across body and down toward front foot	_____	_____
Direction of trunk: flexed and rotated around	_____	_____
Weight shift slightly forward	_____	_____
Back leg and foot automatically move to ready position	_____	_____

Rating scale: 4-very good, 3-good, 2-fair, 1-insufficient (Klatt, 1990)

catch or hold back the throwing arm until the hips, trunk, and finally the upper body come around. Do not release your grasp until the desired rotations have occurred.

What Should the Coach Consider When Using Video to Assess Performance?

The use of video depends upon the amount and type of information you want to acquire. Plan ahead before videotaping, to save time and determine what information you want to record.

Determine specifically *what* you want to identify. What is the purpose of the specific task? Force? Accuracy? Maximum force with control? Determine the direction and time interval of the specific skill. Is the skill performed repetitively, as in running, or is it performed as an all-out effort, as in throwing or hitting?

The skill needs to be viewed in its entirety, from the preparation phase to the completion of the follow-through. Because performance takes place from head to toe, you need to observe complete action of the lower extremity through the trunk, head, and upper extremities. Keep a consistent point of reference in the background throughout the observation.

Video functions at a rate of 30 frames per second, and you can determine how long various movements take by counting frames (each frame is 0.033 seconds). Suppose you find that one player stealing second was in contact with the ground for 10 video frames (10 × 0.033 seconds or

Table 3.2
Fielding Mechanics Analysis

Mechanics (progressive)	Rating	Comments
Preparation/ready position:		
Relaxed and comfortable position	_____	_____
Feet shoulder-width apart, parallel/square stance	_____	_____
Base of support includes entire foot, heels down	_____	_____
Hips, knees, and ankles bent	_____	_____
Trunk straight, slightly inclined forward	_____	_____
Head comfortable, bat level	_____	_____
Shoulders slightly forward; elbows bent 90 degrees	_____	_____
Arms slightly away from body, relaxed	_____	_____
Positioning phase:	_____	_____
First move, shift of weight in direction of ball	_____	_____
Pivot on foot closest to ball, step forward or backward	_____	_____
Head moves in direction of ball off bat	_____	_____
Rapid run to fielding location	_____	_____
Forward/backward foot position, slightly apart	_____	_____
Body directly behind oncoming ball	_____	_____
Reduction of force phase:		
Catch is on throwing side	_____	_____
Fingers appropriately upward or downward	_____	_____
Upon ball contact, hands are pulled into body	_____	_____
Weight shift onto back bent leg, leg on catching side	_____	_____
Trunk rotates to catching side	_____	_____
Transfer of momentum from catch to throw	_____	_____

Rating scale: 4-very good, 3-good, 2-fair, 1-insufficient (Klatt, 1990)

Table 3.3
Batting Mechanics Analyses

Mechanics (progressive)	Rating	Comments
Preparation/stance phase:		
Upright, relaxed stance	_____	_____
Back foot, hips, and shoulders at 90-degree angle to flight line	_____	_____
Body weight over bent back leg (hip, knee, and ankle)	_____	_____
Front foot light-weighted, approximately shoulder-width	_____	_____
Front arm and elbow at top of strike zone	_____	_____
Hands at top of rear shoulder	_____	_____
Bat between horizontal and vertical	_____	_____
Back leg and hip coiled on inside	_____	_____
Force/swing phase:		
Stride forward 8 to 12 inches	_____	_____
Consistency of stride	_____	_____
Center of gravity or body weight shifts forward	_____	_____
Pelvic rotation (belt buckle toward pitcher)	_____	_____
Trunk rotation	_____	_____
Immediate straight front arm (elbow)	_____	_____
Back arm "throws" from inside out	_____	_____
Horizontal-level swing	_____	_____
Head remains stationary with slight adjustment to see ball	_____	_____
Follow-through phase:		
Balanced body position, ground up	_____	_____
Upper body in direction of ball flight	_____	_____
Arm and wrist roll	_____	_____
Full level follow-through; around to opposite side	_____	_____

Rating scale: 4-very good, 3-good, 2-fair, 1-insufficient (Klatt, 1990)

Table 3.4
Running Mechanics Analyses

Mechanics	Rating	Comments
Side view (frontal plane):		
Foot strike (heel, mid, toe)	_____	_____
Slightly bent hip, knee, and ankle	_____	_____
Knee angle approximately 170 degrees at contact	_____	_____
Center of gravity over base of support, braking force	_____	_____
Midsupport phase—lowest center of gravity, knee approximately 145 degrees (may vary up to 170 degrees)	_____	_____
Takeoff (following, highest center of gravity, may vary 4 inches)	_____	_____
Extension of driving hip, knee, and foot	_____	_____
Rear leg kick up	_____	_____
Stride length (longer increasing speed—shorter decreasing speed; consistency; individual optimum)	_____	_____
Length ground contact relative to nonsupport phase (less– greater speed)	_____	_____
Pelvis and shoulder posture (square)	_____	_____
Trunk—straight line (back flat) throughout stride; body lean	_____	_____
Head erect, no strain anterior/ posterior	_____	_____
Rhythmic leg movement (consistency)	_____	_____
Arm action; elbow at approximately 90-degree angle, relaxed; arms working in opposition—balance factor	_____	_____
Relaxed run; jaw easy; all body parts effortless	_____	_____

(Cont.)

Table 3.4
(Continued)

Mechanics	Rating	Comments
Front or rear view (sagittal plane): Foot plant relative to midline—foot forces: inside to outside border, head of metatarsals at time of pushoff	_____	_____
Ankle: pronation in, supination out (right/left)	_____	_____
Knee bows in/out (right/left)	_____	_____
Hip inward/outward rotation, pelvis alignment	_____	_____
Direction of forces, forward/ backward	_____	_____
Head and trunk/spine control, fixed position; arms and legs working together, independent of trunk	_____	_____

Rating scale: 4-very good, 3-good, 2-fair, 1-insufficient (Klatt, 1990)

0.33 seconds), while another maintains ground contact for 20 frames (0.66 seconds). Your conclusion would be that the second runner needs to work on sprinting—he is spending too much time on the ground rather than being airborne.

Where will you shoot the video? Ideally, you want to capture the performer during competition, under the exact conditions in which the skill to be analyzed is meant to be performed. A pitcher might throw 5 miles per hour faster in competition. To compare practice with competition pitching, videotape each. Be sure to take all possible constraints into consideration (e.g., moving objects, reflections, busy background) when selecting your location.

When are you going to videotape? Conditions need to be appropriate for both the player and the videographer. Do it when the time is right both physically and mentally. Weather conditions, lighting, and the direction of the sun may need to be considered.

How are you going to set up for the videotaping? Set up the camera at right angles to the major direction (plane) of action. Place it level on a tripod at about hip height (center of gravity). For noncompetition taping, place a constant background (e.g., a mat) behind the performer to eliminate background interference. Locate the camera at a distance that allows it to record the entire skill; the closer the better, but do not cut off the preparation or follow-through phases. Be sure to view the performance through the viewfinder to test for appropriate distance. Once you have adjusted the camera, including shutter speed, record a short segment focusing on a known length (e.g., a yardstick held either parallel with or perpendicular to the ground) just in case you want known qualities in the future.

One other question you might ask is *how long* (how much)? The purpose of the analysis will determine this. Six to 10 trials, or until you and the player(s) are satisfied and comfortable with the performance, are recommended.

Now you are ready to go immediately to your VCR and observe your quality videography. Watch the skill pattern at regular speed, in slow motion, and frame by frame. VCRs with four heads provide frame-by-frame capabilities. Sit back in a comfortable environment and enjoy analyzing your players' skills through video.

Coaching experts have debated pitching, hitting, fielding, and baserunning techniques for years, bringing forth many theories but never providing complete answers. Reviewing the video alone is not always enough. Deviations of inches and split seconds—which do make a difference—are so small that one cannot discover the discrepancies by just viewing the videotape. Through measurement and quantitative analysis these small differences may be discovered.

Today's technology has made it possible for the coach and biomechanist to analyze any movement from measurements taken from a monitor. Distance and direction (angles) of movement, time relationships, and indirect values of force and velocity may all be ascertained from a video image. Major universities with biomechanics departments have the technology to perform qualitative and quantitative skill analyses (Klatt, 1988) that enable baseball performance to be studied and interpreted in terms of recognizable scientific principles of movement instead of opinions and guesswork.

What Biomechanical Considerations May the Coach Want to Consider to Prevent Injury?

Proper technique, biomechanical principles, and conditioning need to go hand in hand. The hip, knee, and ankle, and the shoulder, elbow, and wrist work as linkage systems. The strengthening of independent body parts, such as the shoulder or the knee or the elbow, has little to do with sport performance.

Because skill patterns are based on force and velocity and the sequencing of joint action, you should condition sport skills as close to gamelike as possible. When working on throwing, consider using a long rope. Extend a 12- to 15-foot rope behind the player. The rope is to be thrown with maximum force; it acts as an extension of body segments and is to be thrown with a whiplike action. Another way to improve throwing (when your player's arm is in good health) is to take a bag of balls and see how far and hard he can throw them, one by one, without a concern for accuracy. Chances of injury are decreased if the whole body (especially the legs, hips, and trunk) is used in throwing, with lesser emphasis and pressure placed on the upper extremity or shoulder. Injuries to the arm are caused by doing "arm" throwing rather than following proper throwing mechanics, which include the legs, hips, and trunk.

When a player throws, his back leg produces forces of 1-1/2 times his body weight. The front leg stride produces forces 2-1/2 times body weight. For conditioning purposes, the body needs to go slightly airborne and return to the ground to get the force of 2 to 3 times body weight. The coiling effect on the inside of the back leg can be developed with a leap/turn exercise. The player leaps from a side-to-the-target stance, executing a 90-degree turn of the body while in the air, and lands with the front leg slightly bent and the front foot pointing toward the target. He then reverses the action, pushing off from the front foot, turning 90 degrees, and landing on the rear foot in its original position. As the alternating leaps are continued, the player should increase the "rotary drive" for each takeoff and the coiling of the legs on each landing. This conditions the stretch reflexes in the legs and produces elastic energy.

Deep lunging and long leaping while maintaining equilibrium are necessary to condition the front or stride leg effectively. For maximum stability, the muscles in front and in back and inside and outside of the leg must all be developed.

Through video analysis it has been determined that a pitcher throws 5 miles per hour faster in a game than during practice. Most of the time this difference comes from the arm rather than the large lower extremities or trunk muscles. Conditioning must include progressive and limited game competition at the beginning of the season, as well as when coming back after time off or from easier game competitions. Practice may have to encourage competition that is force-related and not accuracy-related to maximize whole-body use in throwing.

In the throwing-arm force phase, the front shoulder-joint muscles, as they lengthen in the stretch phase and shorten in the final phase, need to be conditioned. Eccentric (lengthening) contraction movements could be conditioned by using surgical tubing, elastic bands, or other eccentric conditioning machines. A rubber medicine ball thrown against the wall and then caught at shoulder height will put the shoulder on stretch prior to shortening. This conditioning should be done while in the actual throwing position. A reverse position will develop the antagonistic or slow-down muscles used by the arm (Figure 3.13).

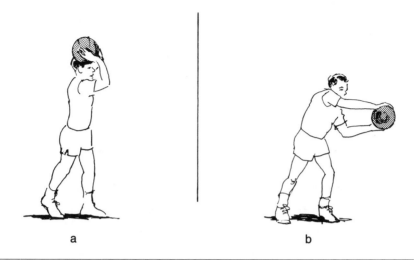

a   b

Figure 3.13 Use of rubber medicine ball to elicit muscle lengthening contraction (eccentric) prior to shortening contraction (concentric). (a) Primary throwing muscles. (b) "Slow-down" (antagonist) throwing muscles.

A note of caution: "If it ain't broke don't fix it!" If the movement is not mechanically incorrect, or if it does not interfere with performance, leave it be. There is a point at which coaching becomes overcoaching.

KEYS TO SUCCESS

- Acquire visual models of the essential skills in baseball. Know and understand effective skill patterns and their differences from idiosyncrasies.

- Observe the action many times from the side, front, or rear, and if possible from above. Be open-minded to remove personal biases.

- Videotape player's skills. Use the enclosed mechanical checklists as a guide.

- Assist your players in analyzing their skills by building on the known and emphasizing one, two, or three major considerations.

- Analyze individual playing skills sequentially from the ground up. The feet determine what the rest of the body can or cannot do when it comes to movement.

- Being centered or in a ready position is critical to success. The ability to move in any direction requires that the center of gravity be directly centered over the base of support.

- Movement depends on the purpose (force or speed) and desired direction of the movement.

- Develop force and speed first, then accuracy. Accuracy is only a slight adjustment at the time of release or contact . . . a little earlier or later, to the right or to the left.

- Body control and good dynamic balance enhance performance and accuracy and prevent injury.

- Develop skill patterns at the speed and range in which they are to be performed.

- Have players practice in situations as gamelike as possible.

- Conditioning must be progressive at all times. Take into consideration lay-overs, weak games, and illness.

- Incorporate fast eccentric and concentric muscle development in practice and conditioning for the lower extremities, trunk, and upper extremities.

- Develop primary movers as well as antagonistic muscles which are used to slow down the action.

- Efficient and proper mechanics will prevent from 80% to 90% of your baseball injuries and you'll enjoy winning more games.

REFERENCES AND RESOURCES

Adrian, M.J., & Cooper, J.M. (1989). *Biomechanics of human movement.* Indianapolis, IN: Benchmark Press.

Atwater, A.E. (1977, May). *Biomechanical analysis of different pitches delivered from the windup and stretch positions.* Paper presented at the 25th Annual Meeting of the American College of Sports Medicine, Chicago, IL.

Breen, J.L. (1967). What makes a good hitter? *Journal of Health, Physical Education, and Recreation, 38,* 36-39.

DeRenne, C. (1989). *A unified approach to optimal performance: Databank.* Lagunas Hills, CA: Bio-Kinetics.

Drysdale, S.J., & Harris, K.S. (1982). *Complete handbook of winning softball.* Boston: Allyn & Bacon.

Graphic design: The art of hitting, pitching, fielding, and managing, (1989, April 24). *Chicago Tribune,* (special insert).

Hay, J.G. (1985). *The biomechanics of sports techniques.* Englewood Cliffs, NJ: Prentice Hall.

Klatt, L.A. (1988). *Kinematic characteristics of throwing and catching.* River Forest, IL: Concordia University.

Klatt, L.A. (1990). *Baseball skill mechanics analysis.* River Forest, IL: Concordia University.

Klatt, L.A., & Calhoun, R. (1988). *The best set position. A position paper.* River Forest, IL: Concordia University.

Kreighbaum, E., & Barthels, K.M. (1990). *Biomechanics: A qualitative approach for studying human movement.* New York: Macmillan.

Schutzler, L.L. (1980). *A cinematographic analysis of stride length in highly skilled baseball pitchers.* Master's thesis, University of Arizona, Tucson.

Slater-Hammel, A.T. (1953). Initial body position and total body reaction time. *Research Quarterly, 24,* 91-96.

CHAPTER 4

Exercise Physiology: Proper Conditioning

Coop DeRenne
University of Hawaii

It's the bottom of the ninth inning. Two outs. The game is tied. Jim Jackson is at bat. On the mound is Will Welch. Welch has pitched magnificently. He takes a no-hitter and a shutout into the last inning. Welch's fastball has been clocked consistently at 88 to 90 miles per hour all night. But during the first two outs of the ninth his velocity has dropped off to 84 to 86 miles per hour.

As Jackson steps to the plate, both the catcher Lioscia and Welch recall Jackson's three previous at-bats—three swinging Ks with not even a loud foul ball. Welch blew Jackson away!

Welch looks in and gets the sign—fastball. As the pitch is delivered, Jackson fouls it off—strike one. Another fouled fastball, and Jackson now is down to his last strike. Jackson is in "no man's land"—can't get any help from anyone. The challenge is set: Welch must try to blow him away.

As the third pitch arrives toward the plate, the noise of the crowd is deafening, drowning out the sound of the bat. The ball jumps off the bat as Jackson stands motionless, witnessing the ball as it clears the center-field fence . . .

Why did Welch fail? We know his fastball decreased 4 to 5 miles per hour during the last inning. Is this decrease enough to make his fastball hittable? Definitely! But why did his fastball lose its velocity?

Maybe Welch was not in good physical condition—his legs might have been too weak due to a lack of proper power weight-training program or an insufficient anaerobic sprint-training conditioning base; or perhaps his stamina was poor because he failed to maintain the right aerobic training level during the competitive season. Or did he outsmart himself—throw the wrong pitch at the wrong time? Welch and his pitching coach, Pete Ivanosk, must find the answer.

Aren't we really asking, Why do athletes succeed and fail? Ever since people began competing athletically, coaches, parents, and players have tried to answer this ageless question. Who has the answer? The answer begins with understanding the importance of a strong fundamental base—*physical conditioning!*

WHY EXERCISE PHYSIOLOGY IS IMPORTANT

Physical conditioning is essential to every baseball program for three important reasons.

First, the correct physical conditioning program can provide a player with the fundamental strength, power, and anaerobic conditioning base he needs to compete successfully at his respective competitive level. At every stage of competitive baseball, from Little League to the big leagues, each successful player has a certain minimum level of strength, power, and stamina. The potential rate for failure is higher for the weaker player who does not reach the minimum level in his respective competitive league.

The second reason exercise physiology is so important is that it gives the coach a strong evaluative base that provides the reference point for determining why athletes succeed or fail. Suppose that, when you evaluate your players' performances, you first diagnose your players' conditioning levels; you will be determining whether your players are hindered by fatigue. Fatigue results from inadequate strength or power (anaerobics). When you evaluate a player's performance, first look at his physical conditioning base and not at his technique level.

You must understand that physical conditioning is the foundation from which all the other human performance sciences draw their relevance and expertise. Human performance sciences have their roots in physical conditioning. It will be easier to use all the other sciences in this evaluative process once the physical conditioning base of each player is established. When the athlete's physical conditioning base is solid, all other human performance sciences will have a stronger impact on the overall total performance of the athlete.

Third, exercise physiology is important because a good physical conditioning program helps reduce injuries. It is well documented that the better conditioned athlete will be less susceptible to major seasonal or career-threatening injuries. His highly conditioned body will be more tolerant of the demands of the game.

Major-league examples of highly conditioned athletes who have had illustrious, long careers because of their physical conditioning lifestyles include these players: Bob Boone (Kansas City Royals), career leader in games and innings caught; Hall of Fame pitcher Tom Seaver; Steve Carlton; and of course fitness fanatic Nolan Ryan. These players are known for their statistical exploits as well as their dedication to physical conditioning.

The bottom line in competitive baseball is the pitcher–hitter confrontation. These two players are on center stage, and the game revolves around their performances. In the Welch versus Jackson confrontation, modern exercise science could have played a major role, for high-tech equipment can be used to assess athletes' physical conditioning levels and provide specific, individualized, research-proven conditioning regimens to prepare them for competition.

EXERCISE PHYSIOLOGY CONCERNS IN BASEBALL

In the clubhouse, in the weight room, and on the field, baseball coaches, strength coaches, parents, and players for years have had four primary misconceptions concerning physical conditioning: (a) that there is a high correlation between body weight and strength, (b) that the terms *strength* and *power* can be interchanged as if they were synonymous, (c) that football-oriented weight training programs are fine for the baseball player, and (d) that physical conditioning for baseball players should be aerobic.

What Is the Correlation Between Strength and Body Weight?

You and your players must understand that there is absolutely no correlation between strength and body weight. The media industry (television, newspapers, magazines, etc.) has indirectly promoted this concept, but just because a player has returned from summer vacation 10 to 15 pounds heavier does not mean he is stronger, more powerful, or faster, with less body fat.

Unless the player has been on an individualized weight training program, his summer body-weight gains may be gains in fat rather than in functional muscle mass, and this would usually reduce his total fitness level. Stress the importance of individualized, baseball-specific summer conditioning programs, and do not target players for unnecessary weight gains.

The physiological fitness components—strength, power, and anaerobic metabolic gains—result from proper weight training, anaerobics, and nutritional training programs. You want a fast and powerful lineup, not heavy, slow, and weak bench-jockeys.

Do Strength and Power Mean the Same Thing?

Strength and *power* are not synonymous terms. Strength and power are created through weight resistance training. Strength is the force a muscle can exert against a resistance. Muscles become stronger when they are systematically subjected to progressively heavier workloads. Therefore, strength will increase when the muscles are forced to work against increasing resistance.

Power, on the other hand, is the rate of producing force (work). Power is the result of *strength* to produce the force and *speed* to increase the rate at which the force can be applied. Simply stated, *power is strength times speed.*

All movement is dynamic in nature. When a player runs, throws, and hits, he is moving over a prescribed distance in a certain amount of time. For the player to move more effectively, he must become more powerful. Why? Because all movement requires a certain level of strength and speed. The combination of strength and speed is *power.*

Baseball is an example of dynamic movements. Baseball therefore is a strength and power-ballistic sport. It involves the velocities of a pitched ball, the high-speed swinging of a bat, and power for sprint running. Strength and power are both weight training qualities essential to executing high-speed ballistic throws, bat swings, running, and stealing bases.

As you can see, the baseball-specific weight training program must include strength training and power training. To develop his power level, the player must first develop a total-body strength base. Then he begins very carefully a specific power-training program. Power training follows strength development in the yearly-cycle weight training program. How you schedule these two training programs in conjunction with the specific anaerobic and aerobic conditioning and technique-development programs is the true measure of your exercise expertise.

Therefore, individualized, specific weight training programs for the pitcher, hitter, and base runner are essential. These weight training programs are extremely different from each other because of the mechanics and demands of the three different positions!

Are Football Weight Training Programs Adequate for Baseball Players?

There is a trend today toward two-sport baseball players in our high schools and youth programs. Traditionally, many baseball players played football in the fall season. This is also the trend today. The coaches who are in charge of the weight training program for football are usually not baseball oriented. These baseball–football players are exposed to harmful non–baseball specific weight training regimens when they play football.

Most popular strength-training exercises (bench presses, squats, military presses, lat bar pull-downs, etc.) are football-oriented and performed in the vertical plane. Baseball basically consists of *rotational* movements performed in the horizontal plane and *lateral* "first two-step quickness" movements. Throwing and hitting are examples of rotational techniques, and defensive fielding is a combination of rotational and lateral movements. According to our specificity of training principle, baseball players must strength- and power-train in the horizontal plane using rotational and lateral movement exercises. Traditional football and popular strength-training exercises do not meet the lateral and rotational demands of the baseball player.

Beware of this negative weight training trend and discuss its potential harms with your school's strength and football coaches.

Is Baseball an Aerobic Activity?

Baseball is not aerobic in nature, yet traditionally most professional and amateur baseball programs use aerobic training to condition their players—having them run lap after lap or mile after mile.

Baseball is an *anaerobic* sport—short, quick, explosive movements of less than 10 seconds' duration. All baseball plays are completed within

10 seconds: hitters exploding out of the batter's box and sprinting around the bases; base stealing; baserunning; defensive players reacting quickly while fielding ground balls and line drives and chasing down long fly balls in the gap; and pitchers ballistically throwing to the catcher.

The energy baseball players use to react in this ballistic game is the result of anaerobic metabolism, which provides the short-term, quick energy source to the cells. All baseball players must condition themselves anaerobically for ballistic power. Baserunners and hitters need to condition their legs for exploding out of the batter's box, for bursting takeoffs while base stealing, and for running around the bases. Pitchers also need to train anaerobically. Pitchers' legs are constantly in motion during the pitch delivery. As Hall of Famer Tom Seaver says as he puts sprinting into proper perspective, "You are only as good as your legs."

Therefore, you must train your players anaerobically through interval training to meet their competitive game demands. Here are some examples of interval training:

1. For the base runners and hitters: daily wind sprints of 10 x 100 yards during the off-season; daily 8-10 x 60 yards during the season; first-step lead-offs base-stealing sprints (5 to 7 repetitions) for reaction time.
2. For the pitcher: daily wind sprints of 10 x 100 yards and optionally mixed in with three alternate days of aerobics for 25 minutes during the off-season; daily wind sprints of 8 x 60 yards and optionally mixed in with 2 or 3 alternate days of aerobics for 25 minutes, or 20 minutes on the stationary bike while icing the arm after pitching.

Don't worry that your players aren't getting enough fitness training. These anaerobic wind sprints will have enough aerobic carryover value. But if you would like to alternate the wind sprints with 25 minutes of aerobics during the week, your training regimen will be less boring and still productive.

You may have the option of using aerobic training with some of your pitchers, if they prefer this kind of training. Three days of 25-minute continuous running per workout is sufficient.

Participating in specific strength and power weight training and anaerobic training programs year-round provides the conditioned player with the proper conditioning base to maximize his athletic abilities. Potentially, the well-conditioned player will be able to come closer to his optimized performance level than the unconditioned athlete. He will have the extra stamina to perform optimally in the late innings as well as over the long season. The highly conditioned athlete will also be able to withstand the demands of the game, reducing the possibilities of seasonal and career-threatening injuries.

What Should I Know About Weight Training?

In this section, principles of exercise are presented that provide you with fundamental information for knowledgeably training your players in the weight room. The most important principle of exercise is specificity of training. All other principles derive their importance from this principle.

Specificity of Training

The principle of specificity of training states that there is a positive transfer of training effect when weight training and anaerobic and aerobic training exercises are performed over ranges of motion (ROMs) that are close or identical to the ROMs of the specific sport skills for which one is training. Therefore, exercises for hitting and pitching must be compatible with the alternating acceleration and deceleration arm movements involved in those skills.

Specificity means that the body adapts to a specific stress by making a specific change that will help the muscle better handle that stress. For example, weight room exercises for batting that duplicate the acceleration and deceleration arm and bat movements will bring about changes that will enable the hitter to hit better.

The hitter not only has to duplicate his sport skill–specific ROM in the weight room, he must exercise at a speed or rate through the specific range of motion close to the competitive game speed. According to the specificity of training principle, it is logical to expect a hitter or pitcher to achieve optimal strength gains by doing his strength-building exercises at the speeds and in the full ROM required during the competitive game.

Specificity exercises for hitters and pitchers must include the following four training conditions: (a) overload, (b) resistance throughout the total ROM, (c) duplication of the acceleration–deceleration (rate of speed) arm patterns of the swing and throw, and (d) safety.

If all four exercise conditions come together in unison during the exercise workout, not only are the muscles themselves being exercised, but neurological changes are being produced. The neurological changes improve the timing of muscle-fiber firing (synchronization) and the number and type of muscle fibers recruited. To produce these neurological changes, hitters and pitchers must exercise at speeds close to or greater than competitive velocities. No single exercise has the acceleration–deceleration and resistance capabilities to produce the muscle-fiber recruiting process needed for performing hitting and throwing movements in a safe and controlled manner.

Periodization Principle

Periodization is the division of the year into different training regimens to meet two specific objectives, those of preparing the athlete for (a) optimal improvement in performance, and (b) a definite climax to the competitive season. Periodization consists of periodic changes of training objectives, tasks, and content, and the training year is divided into the following three periods.

Preparation Period. The first cycle in the general preparatory period is the *base* cycle, which begins in the off-season and lasts for 10 weeks. The focus of this period is to develop the athlete's general fitness base and get the player into shape for the following training cycles. The athlete's weight lifting program emphasizes strength building to hypertrophy (volume) and for prevention of injuries, and it includes many different kinds of exercises for all the major muscles of the body. The players spend only a limited amount of time playing baseball.

For anaerobic training, the players should run-sprint intervals of 30 to 300 yards for approximately 15 to 20 minutes for 3 or 4 days a week. You could mix in base-stealing sprints and technique training at this time. If you train your position players and pitchers in this manner, you will also be satisfying aerobic fitness demands for your players.

The next cycle of the general preparatory period is the specialized preparatory period or *power* cycle, which is also in the off-season and lasts approximately 9 to 12 weeks. Training becomes selective, corresponding to the player's specific sport skill. The volume of work (number of exercises and repetitions) performed decreases, but the intensity and complexity of workouts increases. In other words, the player trains for speed and strength simultaneously. Specifically, the athlete trains explosively for the ballistic movements of hitting, pitching, and baserunning, duplicating these movements in their precise ROMs and at competitive game speeds. Skill work is emphasized during this period. Continue the anaerobic run-sprint interval training sessions.

Maintenance (Competitive) Period. This period lasts throughout the competitive season and emphasizes maintenance of acquired strength and power. Because of the high number of games played over the long season and the different weekly game schedules, weight training should be conducted at least two times per week.

Starting pitchers' and relief pitchers' weight training schedules must be handled with extreme care. When scheduling the pitchers' weight training sessions, give these guidelines to your pitchers:

- Weight train 2 days a week with free weights. You can lift 3 days a week according to the Jobe light-dumbbell range of motion resistance arm exercise program. If possible, do not lift 2 consecutive days.
- If possible, never lift the day before, day of, or day after a game appearance.

- If you are a relief pitcher who may or may not pitch that day, and you want to lift that day, only perform the Jobe light-dumbbell arm exercise program. Lift either early in the morning or after the game.
- Never lift alone. Every lifting session must be supervised.
- All lifting movements must be performed in a *smooth, slow,* and *controlled* fashion throughout the correct ranges of motion.
- Stretch before and after each workout session. Each stretching period should last approximately 15 minutes.

During this training period skill techniques should stabilize, bringing performance to a peak. Your maintenance conditioning and skill refinement programs must peak with the championship phase of your competitive season. Beware that the players are not too fatigued or too weak going into the most important part of your season–the play-offs. The maintenance weight training program must prevent significant losses in strength and power that were developed before the season started. Your anaerobic interval-training program will be reduced to approximately daily 10 x 60-yard run-sprints and 10 base-stealing sprints.

Active Rest (Transitional) Period.   The final training period is a transitional time beginning after the conclusion of the season. This period marks the transition from peak performance into an active rest period lasting 4 weeks. The player participates in supplemental sport activities that will help his specific sport-skill development and will keep the athlete in good cardiovascular condition. This period is also for rehabilitation, with no weight training taking place.

Hitters, for example, should participate in the following visual tracking sports: badminton, Ping-Pong, tennis, and racquetball. They should also exercise aerobically 3 days a week for 25 to 30 minutes per workout session, using one or more of the following sports: swimming, jogging, dance aerobics, and biking.

The Exercise Continuum

The training concept of an exercise continuum works in tandem with the periodization principle. The exercise continuum regulates the strength, power, and flexibility weight training exercises used in the periodization process. This continuum outlines specific programs for hitters, pitchers, and base runners. As the athlete exercises through the continuum, he continually develops his mechanical skills, targeting the championship period for peak performance.

The exercise continuum charts for the pitchers, hitters, and base runners appear at the end of the chapter in figures 4.2, 4.3, and 4.4. The five characteristics of each exercise continuum are as follows:

1. General strength building: free weights and heavy dumbbells.

2. Range-of-motion resistance: light dumbbells—Jobe program.
3. Task-specific resistance: medicine balls, plyometrics, footballs, and stride box.
4. Sport-specific resistance: short/long toss with weighted baseballs, weighted bat swings, and wind sprints.
5. Skill-specific resistance: pitching with weighted baseballs, weighted bat drills, wind sprints, and first step lead-offs.

Principle of Stress Adaptation

Muscle reacts to stress when it is stressed beyond normal demands. If the stress is slightly greater than normal, the muscle responds positively and becomes stronger. For example, during a weight training session, if the intensity of the workout is increased gradually and systematically, the muscles respond positively and gain strength.

Principle of Rebuilding Time

After a muscle is stressed beyond its normal demands, there must be a certain amount of time for the tissues to recover and adapt. With sufficient rest between workouts, the muscle builds to a slightly higher strength level. It is best to rest 48 hours (e.g., exercise M-W-F) between workouts.

Principle of Overload

For the athlete to obtain a maximum training effect, resistance demands must be gradually intensified over an extended period of time. This is the principle of progressive overload.

Physiologists generally agree that weightloads exceeding 75% of maximum are most effective for achieving strength gains. This is because the single most important factor in strength development is the intensity of the training stimulus.

Regardless of the player's maximum weightload in a given exercise, the 10RM (RM = maximum weightload lifted during one repetition) weightload usually corresponds to about 75% of that maximum. In other words, the heaviest weightload the player can lift 10 times in succession is approximately 75% of the maximum weightload he can lift once. Therefore, players who train with 10RM weightloads apply sufficient muscular stress to produce strength gains.

Principle of Controlled Movement Speed

When the athlete is training with free weights, machine weights, and dumbbells, it is important that the weightload be raised and lowered in a slow and controlled manner. This controlled movement provides for a consistent application of force through the exercise ROM.

This controlled movement reduces the possibility of injury because it subjects the muscles to a more or less consistent force-stress level during both the lifting phase (concentric muscle contraction) and the lowering phase (eccentric muscle contraction). As a rule of thumb, the raising of the weightload should take about 1.5 seconds, and the lowering should take about twice as long.

Principle of Full-Range Movements

The athlete must exercise muscles through their full ROM for the following three reasons:

- This will increase or maintain joint flexibility and mobility.
- Full-range movements provide the muscles with a greater training stimulus because the distance over which a muscle moves a weightload is proportional to the amount of work done (work = force x distance). Therefore, the muscle that moves the weightload over the full ROM performs more work than the muscle that executes a partial movement with the same weightload.
- Because baseball skills of throwing, hitting, and sprinting require application of force over the maximum distance possible, performing less than full-range specific exercise movements has limited practical value.

Principle of Muscle Balance

Weight training programs must be designed to promote strength development in all the major muscle groups. If you emphasize training only certain muscle groups, your athletes will produce muscle imbalance and increase the risk of possible injury. They must exercise the joint prime-movers (major muscle groups) and their corresponding antagonistic (opposite side) muscles. For example, the elbow prime-mover is the bicep muscle, and its antagonistic muscle is the tricep.

Weighted Implement Training Principle (Underload/Overload)

Weighted implement training consists of exercising with modified standard competitive implements (bats and baseballs) while duplicating the acceleration–deceleration full ROM for the arm. Hitters and pitchers exercise according to a specific guided-training regimen with specific weighted bats and baseballs close to the competitive lengths and weights.

Hitting Regimen. The player should use the off-season hitting regimen in Table 4.1 three or four times a week during batting practice or in the weight room.

Table 4.1
Hitting Regimen

1. Bat weights: heavy = 31 to 34 ounces
   light = 29 to 27 ounces
   standard = 30 ounces
2. Begin with heavy 31-ounce and light 29-ounce bats.
3. Every three weeks increase heavy bat one ounce (overload) and decrease light bat one ounce (underload). Heavy bat will eventually be 34 ounces, and light bat will be 27 ounces.
4. Bat workout sequence: (a) Warm up with standard bat, (b) hit or swing heavy bat, (c) hit or swing light bat, (d) hit or swing standard bat.
5. Minimum number of bat swings: (a) 25 cuts with standard bat, (b) 50 with heavy bat, (c) 50 with light bat, (d) 50 with standard bat.

Table 4.2
Pitching Regimen

1. Weighted baseballs: heavy = 6 ounces
   light = 4 ounces
   standard = 5 ounces
2. Baseball sequence: (a) Warm up with football 5 to 7 minutes, (b) warm up long toss with 5-6-4-5 baseball sequence (5 to 7 throws per baseball), (c) in bull pen, warm up with 5-ounce baseball, throw heavy baseball, throw light baseball, end workout throwing standard 5-ounce baseball.
3. Number of pitches:
   Option 1: standard-heavy-light-standard sequence:
      weeks 1-3: 54 pitches (9-18-18-9)
      weeks 4-6: 60 pitches (10-20-20-10)
      weeks 7-9: 66 pitches (11-22-22-11)
      weeks 10-12: 75 pitches (12-25-25-13)
   Option 2: first 6 weeks standard-heavy-standard; second 6 weeks standard-light-standard:
      weeks 1-3: 54 pitches (9-36-9)
      weeks 4-6: 60 pitches (10-40-10)
      weeks 7-9: 66 pitches (11-44-11)
      weeks 10-12: 75 pitches (12-50-13)

Pitching Regimen.   The pitcher should use the 12-week off-season bull pen throwing program (two or three times per week) in Table 4.2.

Power Training

The combination of strength and speed training is called power training, and it requires specialized training. Simply stated, power is the product of strength and speed. Power is the ability to apply strength with speed. Where there is movement, there's power. The faster the movement and the greater the resistance to be overcome, the greater the requirement is for power.

The amount of force created by contracting muscles determines how much you lift, how high you jump, and how much explosive speed you generate. The key to training for power is to move as much resistance as possible over a prescribed distance in the shortest time possible. Power is developed through the lifting of heavy weights at fast speeds. The heavy weightload range an athlete can lift at a fast speed and not worry about the possibility of injury is 50% to 60% of his 1RM (maximum weightload lifted with 1 repetition).

In other words, power training means lifting heavy weights fast while exerting a maximum effort to move a load approximately 50% of one's 1RM as fast as possible over the required full ROM. A power training program must include the training guidelines in Table 4.3.

Pyramid Principle

The athlete, when lifting with free weights or machines, must apply the pyramid principle to his lifting technique. During the light, medium, and heavy weightload workout days, the athlete begins lifting upward from a

Table 4.3
Power Training Guidelines

1. Exercise 3 times per week with 48 hours of rest in between (e.g., exercise M-W-F).
2. Use the following strength weightloads for the 3 days of lifting: light day, 50% to 65% of maximum; medium day, 65% to 75% of maximum; heavy day, 80% to 95% of maximum.
3. Do five repetitions per set; three to five sets. Work up in weight, reaching the heaviest weightload on the next-to-last set and drop down in weight on the last set.
4. To develop power in quick movements, do the last three repetitions of the first two sets with the lightest weightloads at maximum speed (50% to 60% of 1RM).
5. Every third week, on the heavy day use weightloads of 90% to 100% of maximum with one to five repetitions.
6. Every third week, on the light day do five sets of five repetitions with weightloads of 40% to 60% of maximum. You should do the fast movements only in the lifts that involve the same muscles and movements used in your skill-specific ROM (specificity of training).
7. During the year-round (periodization) weight training program, the power cycle will follow the strength foundational cycle. This power or speed-strength cycle will last for approximately 3 months.

warm-up set to the highest targeted weightload. Once he achieves the highest weightload at the top of the pyramid, he must lift lighter weightloads, thus working downward in the pyramid.

The player should be very cautious not to "hurdle" (skipping over too many weightload levels) over too many progressive weightload levels when pyramiding. Therefore, the player must systematically pyramid upward to his prescribed targeted weightload ceiling for each workout session. The pyramiding process reduces stress on the connective tissues and reduces the risk of injury. Every type of exercise requires a light warm-up set within each respective exercise.

How Do I Design Training Programs?

In this section, you will read the information necessary to design a training program for your baseball players. This information will be based on the principles of exercise.

Warm-Up

The warm-up, the preactivity exercise for competitive events and daily practices, produces physiological and psychological benefits while decreasing the risk of injuries. Because warm-up routines are athletic and sport-specific, it is important to have a basic understanding of the various techniques and physiological processes involved in warming up.

The traditional warm-up routine, consisting of vigorous exercises combined with flexibility (stretching) activities and followed by sport-specific movements, raises muscle temperature, which in turn facilitates increased contractile force and speed. In athletes who haven't warmed up, the lower muscle temperatures cause a loss in reaction time, a slowing of muscle speed, a loss of muscle stimulation, and an increase in the duration of action potential that can result in muscle injuries, such as strains, pulls, tears, detachments of tendinous origins, or insertions.

A word of caution: stretching routines should be performed after a general warm-up (light jogging) to achieve the best results and reduce the potential risk of stretching-induced injuries.

If the goal of warm-up is to increase local muscle or total body temperatures, then a baseball practice and pregame warm-up sequential program should include the following:

1. General warm-up: jogging, calisthenics, and rope jumping, followed by
2. Sport-specific warm-up:

    a. stretching program
    b. wind sprints

c. football throws to tolerance

d. short/long toss: throwing with standard and weighted baseballs (standard-heavy-light-standard: 5-6-4-5-ounce) by throwing one-hops (never throw a baseball in a lobbing parabola fashion) on a direct line to your partner

All warm-up activities must be conducted in running shoes, not in baseball cleats, to reduce the possibility of injury.

End each workout with a cool-down period of light stretching and walking. This period allows muscles to recover from the strenuous workouts.

Stretching

Stretching should be done slowly, with no bouncing or jerky movements. Stretching exercises should begin with the largest major groups and work upward to the arms and shoulders. Stretch to where you feel a slight, easy comfortable stretch. Hold this feeling of a slight stretch for 15 to 30 seconds, then slowly increase the stretch as you feel yourself relax. Do not strain or hold a stretch that is drastic or painful.

Stretch your muscles slowly and with control, remembering that the key is to be relaxed. Don't worry about flexibility. Stretch relaxed, and your flexibility will increase. The stretches in Figure 4.1 are especially beneficial to baseball players.

(Cont.)

Figure 4.1   Stretching exercises.

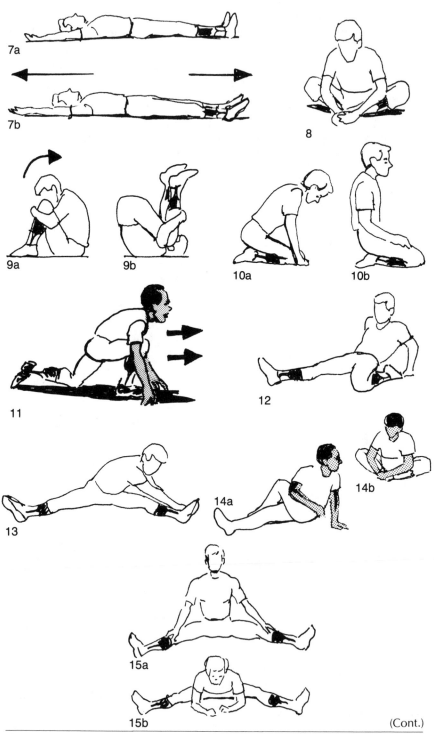

Figure 4.1   (Continued)

(Cont.)

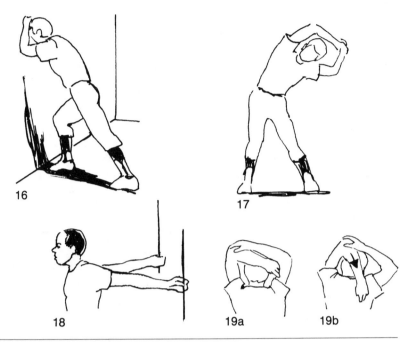

Figure 4.1   (Continued)

Weight Training

There are 10 major muscle groups that must be exercised for strength and power development, listed here in the proper weight lifting sequence:

1. Chest
2. Back
3. Shoulders
4. Triceps
5. Biceps
6. Midsection
7. Quadriceps
8. Hamstrings
9. Lower legs
10. Forearms

Number of Exercises.   Select a small number of exercises that involve all the major muscle groups. For example, the bench press, power clean, and full squat are sufficient training exercises for most of the major muscle groups. Add a few supplemental exercises that are skill-specific, and you have the makings of a proven specificity weight training program.

Paired Exercises.   To promote muscle balance, flexibility, and injury-free training, the athlete should exercise both the prime-mover muscles and their antagonistic muscles—for example, biceps with triceps.

Exercise Variation. It is important to have several exercise variations for each prime-mover muscle group. Frequent changes in the training routine are necessary for the sake of variety, but one needn't perform more than two separate exercises per workout for a specific muscle group.

Time of Day. The time of day at which the athlete trains does not significantly affect the training process. You should give your players at least 2 hours to recover from the weight training workout before daily practices, so weight training should be done early in the day, preferably in the morning before classes, or in between classes before lunch.

Players should avoid exercising after heavy meals. The digestive process is delayed then and would cause discomfort during the training period.

Frequency. Most exercise scientists and physiologists recommend a 3-alternate-day strength and power training schedule (M-W-F). This schedule allows the athlete more than adequate rest for the tissue-rebuilding process.

Training Time. Most exercise scientists suggest a 40-minute workout in which 15 sets of exercise are completed. The workout should be relatively brief and intense. Time spent socializing, stretching, warming up, and cooling down should not be counted as workout time.

The 40-minute suggested total time might seem too short to you. But remember, you do not want to diminish the athlete's total energy in the weight room and have little left for practices or games. Light is right, in season!

Sets. For strength development, three to six sets per exercise have proven most productive. Not all exercises require the same number of sets during the workout. Fewer sets could be executed when exercising the antagonistic muscles groups than when exercising the prime movers.

Repetitions. You have some flexibility as to the number of repetitions a competitive athlete should perform as he trains for optimum strength. For optimum strength, fewer than 10 maximum repetitions should be used, with a minimum of 70% to 85% of the 1RM. Lifting 10 to 15 repetitions per set builds muscle mass. If the athlete pumps more than 15 repetitions for any exercise, he is entering the endurance area.

Rest Intervals. Remember that there is a certain amount of time needed for the tissues to recover from weight lifting (the rebuilding principle). You must understand the following rest interval principles:

- The quantity and quality of the rest interval is responsible for the repair and growth of muscle tissues.
- The basic function of the recovery period is to allow the stressed and fatigued muscle tissues to rebuild to a higher level of strength.

- Muscle growth occurs between training sessions.
- The length of the rest period is proportional to the length of the training session. Therefore, the advanced weight lifter needs more rest than the novice weight lifter.

Forty-eight hours of rest between workout sessions, with three training periods (M-W-F) per week during the off-season, is required. In season, two to three maintenance training sessions per week are sufficient.

Energy stores in the muscles are replenished after submaximum or maximum effort within 3 minutes following the strenuous exercise bout. Rest periods greater than 3 minutes do not significantly increase the energy stores. A full recovery of 3 minutes is needed to increase muscle strength.

If an athlete is performing circuit training exercises while lifting only one set per exercise, the rest interval can be shortened if successive exercises do not stress the same major muscle groups. A 1-minute rest interval is sufficient between circuit training exercises.

Breathing.   The proper lifting of a weightload is based on two major safety factors: inhaling and exhaling with every repetition, and keeping the weight moving throughout every repetition.

The athlete must breathe on every repetition. He must inhale while lowering the weight and exhale while raising it. Always make sure the player keeps his mouth open to equalize the pressure in the chest cavity.

Training Equipment.   In the last 20 years, the commercial athletic industry has produced a great variety of equipment for the recreator and the serious athlete, and scientists have conducted numerous research studies to determine which types of equipment are best suited for specific sport-skill requirements.

Baseball is a ballistic sport—involving throwing, hitting, and sprinting—and the training equipment you select must develop total body strength and power throughout the joints' ROMs. I recommend the following:

1. Free weights and dumbbells: These offer greater freedom of movement and strengthen the joints.
2. Machines: Have your athletes use these only when there is a constant-resistance weightload so they can explode for power (ballistic action) as well as train for strength.
3. Weighted implement training (overloading and underloading): Train with heavy-light-standard baseball bats and weighted baseballs.

Exercise Sequence.   It is most desirable to train early in the workout with those exercises that use the heavier weightloads. These exercises involve the larger muscles groups, such as the chest, back, and legs.

It is recommended that the athlete alternate muscle groups when performing successive exercises, as this reduces the risk of injury while developing more strength and power.

Exercise Speed. Here is a summary of our earlier discussion of the importance of speed in strength and power development:

- Training for strength: Use slow and controlled movements.
- Training for power: Explosive movements are recommended with 50% to 60% of 1RM. Plyometric training—depth box jumps, lateral leg jumps, single-leg bounds, and rope jumping. Medicine ball twisting exercises. After 3 months of strength development, train approximately 3 months for power.
- Weighted implement training (overload and underload): Use precision-weighted baseballs and bats, and program guidelines, in a supplementary ballistic weight training regimen.
- Circuit training: These exercises should be aerobic. Each exercise should be 45 seconds (15 to 20 repetitions) with a 1-minute rest interval between exercises. Set up the sequence alternating upper body and lower body exercises. If possible, athletes should never execute two arm exercises in a row. If a player is circuit training by himself, he should execute a warm-up set before lifting the prescribed weightload at each exercise station.

Weight Training Exercises. Every baseball weight training program is unique in terms of number of players to be trained, budget, time, facilities, and equipment. See Table 4.4 for equipment exercise suggestions. It is hoped that your program has the equipment necessary to exercise all your players according to the exercise principles.

Injury Prevention. You must give your players information on injury prevention. You can help players reduce injuries by educating them in the principles of exercise and teaching them proper lifting techniques and resting principles. Players should be taught to heed warning signs of potential trouble when fatigued. Remember that most training-related injuries occur during the last few repetitions of the final set, when the athlete is most fatigued. Here are some helpful hints to give your players to reduce the risk of injury:

1. Stretch before and after each workout session.
2. Warm up thoroughly before exercising, with no more than 50% of your 1RM.
3. Stop lifting when you can no longer maintain absolute training form or technique.
4. Avoid ballistic movements with excessively heavy weightloads, which could tear ligaments and tendon tissues, particularly near the end of a movement.

Table 4.4
Weight Training Exercise

Universal Gym	Nautilus	Free weights: The Big Three*
1. Chest: bench press	1. Chest: decline press, bent arm fly (double chest machine)	1. Barbell supine bench press
2. Back: lat bar pull-down, bar dips	2. Back: pullover and lat bar pull-down (duo-poly pullover machine)	2. Full back squats
3. Shoulders: upright row, overhead press	3. Shoulders: side lateral raise (double shoulder machine)	3. Power clean
4. Triceps: press-down (lat bar)	4. Triceps: triceps extension (biceps-triceps machine	Substitutes to Big Three:
5. Biceps: standing curl	5. Biceps: biceps curl	A. Dumbbell bench press
6. Midsection: twisting trunk curls	6. Quadriceps: leg extension, leg press	B. Back lat pull-down
7. Quadriceps: leg extension (press)	7. Hamstrings: leg curl (leg curl machine)	C. Vertical leg press, plyometrics—depth jumps
8. Hamstrings: leg curls, depth jumps	8. Lower legs: heel raise (multi-exercise machine)	
9. Lower leg: leaper machine, toe raises	9. Forearms: wrist curl (multi-exercise machine)	
10. Forearms: wrist curls, reverse curls	10. Neck: neck extension and flexion (four-way neck machine)	

*The Big Three exercise all the major prime-mover muscle groups.

5. Be sure to use spotters when exercising with heavy weightloads, especially during the bench press and squat exercises.
6. Take the full 3 minutes' rest period between exercises.
7. Train 3 days a week, with a rest day between training sessions: M-W-F; T-TH-S.

Steroids: A Word of Caution. You must warn your players against the harmful use of steroids. Steroids work! They will add artificial strength and muscle mass to your players' bodies. But these drugs also produce harmful side effects to the internal organs.

Strength Plateaus. When an athlete finds that his strength progress comes to a halt during the training year, he is experiencing a strength plateau. The player's strength gains have leveled off.

A strength plateau is an indication that some aspect of the training program should be changed. Most athletes invariably choose to work harder in an attempt to increase strength development. This seldom works. The better alternative is to reduce the workout demands to allow the muscle recovery and building processes to catch up. Schedule more recovery time between workouts. If this does not work, consider changing the exercise routine. Changing the routine can be done in the following ways:

- Alter the exercise intensity (sets and repetitions); reduce the total number of sets and repetitions.
- Switch training programs.
- Switch training exercises and equipment.
- Cut down training days and add aerobics. The more efficient the cardiovascular system, the better the muscles will adapt to higher intensity levels.

PUTTING PHYSIOLOGY TO WORK FOR YOU

This section contains specific pitching, hitting, and baserunning conditioning programs. These three conditioning models are based on the latest exercise science research and equipment developments.

Each conditioning model begins with a specific exercise continuum chart that gives players an overview of the specific conditioning program. The succeeding charts in each conditioning model are the specific periodization-training program examples for the entire year. (See Figures 4.2, 4.3, and 4.4.)

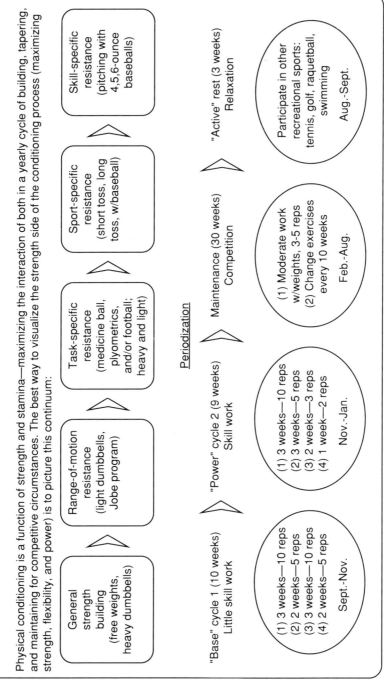

Pitchers' Exercise Continuum

Physical conditioning is a function of strength and stamina—maximizing the interaction of both in a yearly cycle of building, tapering, and maintaining for competitive circumstances. The best way to visualize the strength side of the conditioning process (maximizing strength, flexibility, and power) is to picture this continuum:

General strength building (free weights, heavy dumbbells)

Range-of-motion resistance (light dumbbells, Jobe program)

Task-specific resistance (medicine ball, plyometrics, and/or football; heavy and light)

Sport-specific resistance (short toss, long toss, w/baseball)

Skill-specific resistance (pitching with 4,5,6-ounce baseballs)

Periodization

"Base" cycle 1 (10 weeks)
Little skill work

(1) 3 weeks—10 reps
(2) 2 weeks—5 reps
(3) 3 weeks—10 reps
(4) 2 weeks—5 reps

Sept.-Nov.

"Power" cycle 2 (9 weeks)
Skill work

(1) 3 weeks—10 reps
(2) 3 weeks—5 reps
(3) 2 weeks—3 reps
(4) 1 week—2 reps

Nov.-Jan.

Maintenance (30 weeks)
Competition

(1) Moderate work w/weights, 3-5 reps
(2) Change exercises every 10 weeks

Feb.-Aug.

"Active" rest (3 weeks)
Relaxation

Participate in other recreational sports: tennis, golf, raquetball, swimming

Aug.-Sept.

Figure 4.2 Physical conditioning for pitchers.

(Cont.)

Pitchers' Training Program for "Base" Cycle 1

Program prepared for _____

Week 1 2 3 6 7 8 : one set per exercise
Week 4 5 9 10 : two sets per exercise

Monday

Exercise	Reps	lb	Total
1) Wide-grip bench press	10 x		=
2) Wide-grip bent rowing	10 x		=
3) Lying triceps press	10 x		=
4) Biceps curl	10 x		=
5) Dumbbell press	10 x		=
6) Shoulder laterals	10 x		=
7) Barbell T-bench press	10 x		=
8) Medium-stance squats	10 x		=
9) Abdominal curl-ups	10 x		=
10) Forearms (optional)	10 x		=
11) Wind sprints (10 x 100 yd)	10 x		=

Day total = _____

Wednesday

Exercise	Reps	lb	Total
1) Medium-stance squats	10 x		=
2) Wide-grip high pulls	10 x		=
3) Wide-grip shrugs	10 x		=
4) Back extensions	10 x		=
5) Abdominal curl-ups	10 x		=
6) Dumbbell chest flys	10 x		=
7) Wide-grip lat pulls to chest	10 x		=
8) Shoulder laterals	10 x		=
9) Forearms (optional)	10 x		=
10) Wind sprints (10 x 100 yd)	10 x		=

Day total = _____

Friday (85% of Monday)

Exercise	Reps	lb	Total
1) Wide-grip bench press	10 x		=
2) Wide-grip bent rowing	10 x		=
3) Lying triceps curl	10 x		=
4) Biceps curl	10 x		=
5) Dumbbell press	10 x		=
6) Shoulder laterals	10 x		=
7) Barbell T-bench press	10 x		=
8) Abdominal curl-ups	10 x		=
9) Forearms (optional)	10 x		=
10) Wind sprints (10 x 100 yd)	10 x		=

Day total = _____

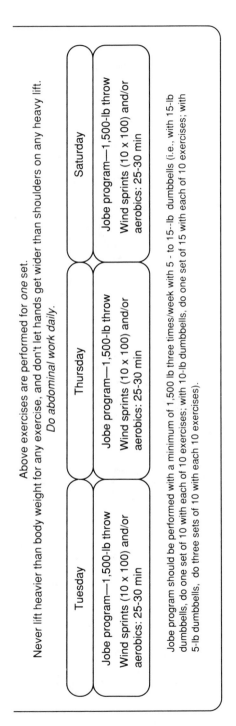

Above exercises are performed for *one* set.

Never lift heavier than body weight for any exercise, and don't let hands get wider than shoulders on any heavy lift.

Do abdominal work daily.

Tuesday	Thursday	Saturday
Jobe program—1,500-lb throw	Jobe program—1,500-lb throw	Jobe program—1,500-lb throw
Wind sprints (10 x 100) and/or aerobics: 25-30 min	Wind sprints (10 x 100) and/or aerobics: 25-30 min	Wind sprints (10 x 100) and/or aerobics: 25-30 min

Jobe program should be performed with a minimum of 1,500 lb three times/week with 5 - to 15--lb dumbbells (i.e., with 15-lb dumbbells, do one set of 10 with each of 10 exercises; with 10-lb dumbbells, do one set of 15 with each of 10 exercises; with 5-lb dumbbells, do three sets of 10 with each 10 exercises).

(Cont.)

Figure 4.2 (Continued)

Pitchers' Training Program for "Power" Cycle 2

Program prepared for _____

Week 1 2 3 : one set per exercise
Week 4 5 6 : two sets per exercise
Week 7 8 : three sets per exercise
Week 9 : five sets per exercise

Monday

Exercise	Reps	lb	Total
1) Dumbbell bench press	10 x	___	= ___
2) Dumbbell bent rowing	10 x	___	= ___
3) Close-grip 6" bench press	10 x	___	= ___
4) Supinating dumbbell curl	10 x	___	= ___
5) Dumbbell press	10 x	___	= ___
6) Shoulder laterals	10 x	___	= ___
7) Dumbbell T-bench press	10 x	___	= ___
8) Wide-stance outside squats	10 x	___	= ___
9) Abdominal curl-ups	10 x	___	= ___
10) Forearms (optional)	10 x	___	= ___
11) Wind sprints (10 x 100 yd)	10 x	___	

Day total = _____

Wednesday

Exercise	Reps	lb	Total
1) Wide-stance outside squats	10 x	___	= ___
2) Medium-grip high pulls	10 x	___	= ___
3) Medium-grip shrugs	10 x	___	= ___
4) Back extensions	10 x	___	= ___
5) Abdominal curl-ups	10 x	___	= ___
6) Dumbbell chest flys	10 x	___	= ___
7) Medium-grip lat pulls to chest	10 x	___	= ___
8) Shoulder laterals	10 x	___	= ___
9) Forearms (optional)	10 x	___	= ___
10) Wind sprints (10 x 100 yd)	10 x	___	

Day total = _____

Friday (85% of Monday)

Exercise	Reps	lb	Total
1) Dumbbell bench press	10 x	___	= ___
2) Dumbbell bent rowing	10 x	___	= ___
3) Close-grip 6" bench press	10 x	___	= ___
4) Supinating dumbbell curl	10 x	___	= ___
5) Dumbbell press	10 x	___	= ___
6) Shoulder laterals	10 x	___	= ___
7) Dumbbell T-bench press	10 x	___	= ___
8) Abdominal curl-ups	10 x	___	= ___
9) Forearms (optional)	10 x	___	= ___
10) Wind sprints (10 x 100 yd)	10 x	___	

Day total = _____

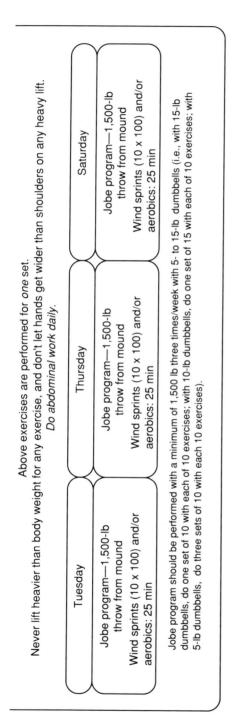

Above exercises are performed for *one* set.

Never lift heavier than body weight for any exercise, and don't let hands get wider than shoulders on any heavy lift.

Do abdominal work daily.

Tuesday	Thursday	Saturday
Jobe program—1,500-lb throw from mound	Jobe program—1,500-lb throw from mound	Jobe program—1,500-lb throw from mound
Wind sprints (10 x 100) and/or aerobics: 25 min	Wind sprints (10 x 100) and/or aerobics: 25 min	Wind sprints (10 x 100) and/or aerobics: 25 min

Jobe program should be performed with a minimum of 1,500 lb three times/week with 5- to 15-lb dumbbells (i.e., with 15-lb dumbbells, do one set of 10 with each of 10 exercises; with 10-lb dumbbells, do one set of 15 with each of 10 exercises; with 5-lb dumbbells, do three sets of 10 with each 10 exercises).

(Cont.)

Figure 4.2 (Continued)

Pitcher's Training Program for Maintenance (in Season)

Program prepared for _____

First and third 10 weeks		Second 10 weeks	
Day 1	Day 2	Day 1	Day 2
1) Squats (1/4) medium stance	1) Squats, medium stance	1) Outside shoulder stance squats	1) Outside-stance squats
2) Wide-grip bench press	2) Wide-grip high pulls	2) Dumbbell bench press	2) Medium-grip shrugs
3) Wide-grip bent rowing	3) Biceps curl	3) Dumbbell bent rowing	3) Dumbbell press
4) Dumbbell press	4) Lying triceps press	4) Shoulder laterals	4) Twist curls
5) Back extensions	5) Shoulder laterals	5) Back extensions	5) Close-grip bench press
6) Abdominal curl-ups	6) Barbell T-bench press	6) Abdominal curl-ups	6) Dumbbell T-bench press
7) Forearms (optional)	7) Abdominal curl-ups	7) Forearms (optional)	7) Abdominal curl-ups
	8) Forearms (optional)		8) Forearms (optional)

Starters lift day before and day after skill work day.
Relievers lift day one, day two, rest a day, and repeat cycle.
Intensity for entire maintenance program is approximately 70% to 85% for all exercises.
Three sets of three to five repetitions are used for all exercises.
Never lift heavier than body weight for any exercise, and don't let hands get wider than shoulders on any heavy lift.
Do abdominal work daily.

Plus: Jobe program and aerobic and anaerobic work to complement same workload:
Wind sprints (8-10 x 60 yards) and 20 minutes on bike while icing arm

Jobe program should be performed with a minimum of 1,500 lb three times/week with 5- to 15-lb dumbbells (i.e., with 15-lb dumbbells, do one set of 10 with each of 10 exercises; with 10-lb dumbbells, do one set of 15 with each of 10 exercises; with 5-lb dumbbells, do three sets of 10 with each 10 exercises).

Figure 4.2 (Continued)

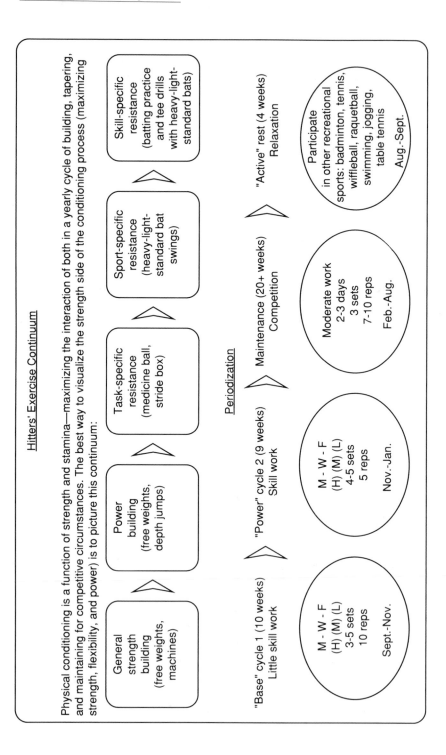

Hitters' Exercise Continuum

Physical conditioning is a function of strength and stamina—maximizing the interaction of both in a yearly cycle of building, tapering, and maintaining for competitive circumstances. The best way to visualize the strength side of the conditioning process (maximizing strength, flexibility, and power) is to picture this continuum:

General strength building (free weights, machines)

Power building (free weights, depth jumps)

Task-specific resistance (medicine ball, stride box)

Sport-specific resistance (heavy-light-standard bat swings)

Skill-specific resistance (batting practice and tee drills with heavy-light-standard bats)

Periodization

"Base" cycle 1 (10 weeks) Little skill work

"Power" cycle 2 (9 weeks) Skill work

Maintenance (20+ weeks) Competition

"Active" rest (4 weeks) Relaxation

M - W - F (H) (M) (L) 3-5 sets 10 reps

Sept.-Nov.

M - W - F (H) (M) (L) 4-5 sets 5 reps

Nov.-Jan.

Moderate work 2-3 days 3 sets 7-10 reps

Feb.-Aug.

Participate in other recreational sports: badminton, tennis, wiffleball, raquetball, swimming, jogging, table tennis

Aug.-Sept.

Hitters' Training Program for "Base" Cycle 1
(10 weeks)

Monday (Heavy day)

Exercise	Sets	Reps	Load*
1) Bench press	5	3-5	85%-100%
2) Lat bar pull or upright rows	3-5	5-7	
3) Depth jumps	3	fatigue	
4) Trunk twists	3	50	
5) Wrist rolls	5	10	
6) Jump rope	5	fatigue	
7) Weighted bats	150	50-50-50	
swings: H L St			

Wednesday (Medium day)

Exercise	Sets	Reps	Load*
1) Bench press	4	7	75%-85%
2) Power cleans	4	7	75%-85%
3) Full squats	4	7	75%-85%
4) Bent-knee twisting sit-ups	4	50	
5) Wrist rolls	4	10	
6) Jump rope	4	fatigue	
7) Weighted bats	150	50-50-50	
swings: H L St			

Friday (Light day)

Exercise	Sets	Reps	Load*
1) Bench press	3	10	60%-75%
2) Power cleans	3	10	60%-75%
3) Full squats	3	10	60%-75%
4) Trunk twists	3	50	
5) Wrist rolls	3	10	
6) Jump rope	3	fatigue	
7) Weighted bats	150	50-50-50	
swings: H L St			

*Load is the percentage weightload of your 1RM (maximum repetition).
Weighted bats sequence is always heavy—light—standard, after warming up with standard bat.

Tuesday

Weighted bat swings
Wind sprints
First-step lead-offs

Thursday

Weighted bat swings
Wind sprints
First-step lead-offs

Saturday

Weighted bat swings
Wind sprints
First-step lead-offs

(Cont.)

Figure 4.3 Physical conditioning for hitters.

Hitters' Training Program for "Power" Cycle 2
(9 weeks)

Monday (Heavy day)

Exercise	Sets	Reps	Load*
1) Bench press	3	5	60%-75%
2) Power cleans	3	5	60%-75%
3) Plyometrics (depth jumps)	3	5	60%-75%
4) Medicine ball bat swings	3	10	
5) Sit-ups-twist	3	100	
6) Wrist rolls	3	10	
7) Jump rope	3	fatigue	
8) Speedbag	3	fatigue	
9) Weighted bats	225 swings: 75-75-75 (H) (L) (S)		
	Weeks 7-9: 300 swings: 100-100-100 (H) (L) (S)		

Wednesday (Medium day)

Exercise	Sets	Reps	Load*
1) Bench press	4	5	50%-60%
2) Power cleans	4	5	50%-60%
3) Plyometrics (depth jumps)	4	5	
4) Medicine ball bat swings	4	10	
5) Sit-ups-twist	4	100	
6) Wrist rolls	4	10	
7) Jump rope	4	fatigue	
8) Speedbag	4	fatigue	
9) Weighted bats	225 swings: 75-75-75 (H) (L) (S)		
	Weeks 7-9: 300 swings: 100-100-100 (H) (L) (S)		

Friday (Light day)

Exercise	Sets	Reps	Load*
1) Bench press	5	5	40%-50%
2) Lat bar pull or upright rows	5	5	40%-50%
3) Depth jumps	3-5	fatigue	
4) Back extensions	3	10	
5) Medicine ball bat swings	5	10	
6) Sit-ups-twist	5	100	
7) Wrist rolls	5	10	
8) Jump rope	5	fatigue	
9) Speedbag	5	fatigue	
10) Weighted bats	225 swings: 75-75-75 (H) (L) (S)		
	Weeks 7-9: 300 swings: 100-100-100 (H) (L) (S)		

*Load is the percentage weightload of your 1 RM (maximum repetition).

Weighted bats sequence is always heavy—light—standard, after warming up with standard bat.

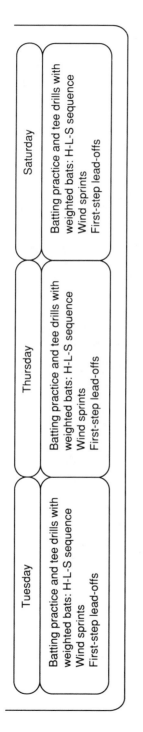

Figure 4.3 (Continued)

(Cont.)

Hitters' Training Program for Maintenance (in Season)
(20+ weeks)

Day 1 (Light day)

Exercise	Sets	Reps	Load*
1) Bench press	3	10	60%-70%
2) Lat pull-down or upright rows	3	10	60%-70%
3) Depth jumps	3		50% effort
4) Medicine ball bat swings	3	10	
5) Weighted bats	150 swings: 50-50-50		
	(H) (L) (S)		

Day 2 (Medium day)

Exercise	Sets	Reps	Load*
1) Bench press	4	7	65%-75%
2) Lat pull-down or upright rows	4	7	65%-75%
3) Depth jumps	4		50% effort
4) Medicine ball bat swings	4	7	
5) Weighted bats	150 swings: 50-50-50		
	(H) (L) (S)		

Day 3 (optional) (Light day)

Same exercise program as day 1

*Load is the percentage weightload of your 1RM (maximum repetition).
Weighted bats sequence is always heavy—light—standard, after warming up with standard bat.
Medicine ball exercise: Done in stride box; simulates swinging; three players in drill.

Plus: Wind sprints
First-step lead-offs

Figure 4.3 (Continued)

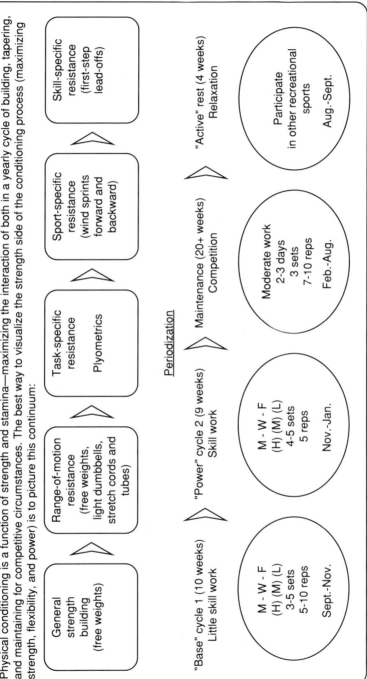

Figure 4.4 Physical conditioning for base runners.

(Cont.)

Baserunners' Training Program for "Base" Cycle 1
(10 weeks)

Monday (Heavy day)

Exercise	Sets	Reps	Load*
1) Bench press	5	3-5	85%-100%
2) Lat pull-downs	3-5	5-7	85%-100%
3) Power cleans	5	3-5	85%-100%
4) Full squats	5	3-5	85%-100%
5) Quadriceps extensions	5	3-5	85%-100%
6) Hamstring curls	5	3-5	85%-100%
7) Jump rope		fatigue	
8) Wind sprints	10 x 100 yd	10-15 min	
9) First-step lead-offs		7-10 reps	

Wednesday (Medium day)

Exercise	Sets	Reps	Load*
1) Bench press	4	7	75%-85%
2) Lat pull-downs	4	7	75%-80%
3) Power cleans	4	7	75%-85%
4) Full squats	4	7	75%-85%
5) Quadriceps extensions	4	7	75%-85%
6) Hamstring curls	4	7	
7) Jump rope		fatigue	
8) Wind sprints	10 x 100 yd	10-15 min	
9) First-step lead-offs		7-10 reps	

Friday (Light day)

Exercise	Sets	Reps	Load*
1) Bench press	3	10	60%-75%
2) Lat pull-downs	3	10	60%-75%
3) Power cleans	3	10	60%-75%
4) Full squats	3	10	60%-75%
5) Quadriceps extensions	3	10	60%-75%
6) Hamstring curls	3	10	60%-75%
7) Jump rope		fatigue	
8) Wind sprints	10 x 100 yd	10-15 min	
9) First-step lead-offs		7-10 reps	

*Load is the percentage weightload of your 1RM (maximum repetition).

Tuesday

Wind sprints: Forward and backward 10 x 100 yd in 10-15 min

First-step lead-off drills for reaction: 7-10 reps

Thursday

Wind sprints: Forward and backward 10 x 100 yd in 10-15 min

First-step lead-off drills for reaction: 7-10 reps

Saturday

Wind sprints: Forward and backward 10 x 100 yd in 10-15 min

First-step lead-off drills for reaction: 7-10 reps

Baserunners' Training Program for "Power" Cycle 2
(9 weeks)

Monday (Heavy day)

Exercise	Sets	Reps	Load*
1) Bench press	5	5	50%
2) Power cleans	5	5	50%
3) Plyometrics	1	10	
4) Quadriceps extensions	5	5	50%
5) Hamstring curls	5	5	50%
6) Jump rope		5 min	
8) Wind sprints	10 x 100 yd 10-15 min		

Wednesday (Medium day)

Exercise	Sets	Reps	Load*
1) Bench press	4	5	40%-50%
2) Power cleans	4	5	40%-50%
3) Plyometrics	1	10	
4) Quadriceps extensions	4	5	40%-50%
5) Hamstring curls	4	5	40%-50%
6) Jump rope		5 min	
8) Wind sprints	10 x 100 yd 10-15 min		

Friday (Light day)

Exercise	Sets	Reps	Load*
1) Bench press	3	5	30%-50%
2) Power cleans	3	5	30%-50%
3) Plyometrics	1	10	
4) Quadriceps extensions	3	5	30%-50%
5) Hamstring curls	3	5	30%-50%
6) Jump rope		5 min	
8) Wind sprints	10 x 100 yd 10-15 min		

Tuesday

Wind sprints: Forward and backward
10 x 100 yd in 10-15 min

First-step lead-off drills for reaction:
7-10 reps

Thursday

Wind sprints: Forward and backward
10 x 100 yd in 10-15 min

First-step lead-off drills for reaction:
7-10 reps

Saturday

Wind sprints: Forward and backward
10 x 100 yd in 10-15 min

First-step lead-off drills for reaction:
7-10 reps

(Cont.)

Figure 4.4   (Continued)

Baserunners' Training Program for Maintenance (in Season)
(20+ weeks)

Monday (Day 1) (Light day)

Exercise	Sets	Reps	Load
1) Bench press	3	10	60%-70%
2) Lat pull-down	3	10	60%-70%
3) Plyometrics	1	10	
4) Jump rope		5 min	
5) Wind sprints	8 x 60 yd		
6) First-step lead-offs		5-7 reps	

Wednesday (Day 2) (Medium day)

Exercise	Sets	Reps	Load
1) Bench press	4	7-10	65%-75%
2) Lat pull-down	4	7-10	65%-75%
3) Plyometrics	1	10	
4) Jump rope		5 min	
5) Wind sprints	8 x 60 yd		
6) First-step lead-offs		5-7 reps	

Friday (optional) (Light day)

Same exercise program as day 1

Tuesday

Wind sprints: Forward and backward
8 x 60 yd

First-step lead-off drills for reaction:
5-7 reps

Wednesday

Wind sprints: Forward and backward
8 x 60 yd

First-step lead-off drills for reaction:
5-7 reps

Friday

Wind sprints: Forward and backward
8 x 60 yd

First-step lead-off drills for reaction:
5-7 reps

Figure 4.4   (Continued)

KEYS TO SUCCESS

- The proper physical conditioning program provides your players with at least the minimal strength, power, and anaerobic capacities they need to compete successfully at their baseball level.

- Your physical conditioning program *must* be specific and train your player for all his specific baseball skills.

- Divide the year-round training program into specific regimens preparing the players to reach their optimum performances during the competitive season with a carryover into the play-offs.

- Once you begin training the players from a general foundation to a more specific plateau, your players will arrive exactly at their peak physical and technique training levels during the competitive season.

- The underloaded and overloaded bats and baseballs and their programs should be incorporated into the periodization conditioning program.

- Physical conditioning is the reference point for evaluating why players succeed or fail.

- Physical conditioning helps reduce seasonal and career-threatening injuries.

- There is no correlation between strength and body weight.

RESOURCES

Anthony, C.P., & Kolthoff, N.J. (1971). *Textbook of anatomy and physiology*. St. Louis, MO: Mosby.

Barnard, R.J. (1976). The heart needs warm-up time. *The Physician and Sportsmedicine, 4,* 9.

Berger, R.A. (1984). *Introduction to weight training*. Englewood Cliffs, NJ: Prentice Hall.

Berger, R.A. (1985, April). The micro-sources of power. *Sports Fitness,* 70-73, 118.

Bush, J. (1988). *Running and baseball videotape*. Los Angeles, CA: Star Quality Sports.

Costill, D., King, D., Holdren, H., & Hargreaves, M. (1983). Sprint speed: U.S. swimming power. *Swimming Technique, 5,* 20-22.

Craig, A., Jr., Boomer, W., & Gibbons, J. (1979). Use of stroke rate, distance per stroke, and velocity relationships in training for competitive swimming. In J. Terauds & E. Bedingfield (Eds.), *Swimming III* (pp. 163-172). Baltimore: University Park Press.

Delorme, T.L., & Watkins, A. (1948). Techniques of progressive resistance exercise. *Archives of Physical Medicine, 29*, 263-273.

DeRenne, C. (1987). Implement weight training programs. *National Strength Coaches Association Journal, 9*, 3, 35-37.

DeRenne, C. (1982, March). Increasing bat velocity. *Athletic Journal*, 28-31.

DeRenne, C., Ho, K., & Blitzblaus, A. (1990). Effects of weighted implement training on throwing velocity. *Journal of Applied Sport Science Research, 4*(1), 16-19.

DeRenne, C., & Okasaki, E. (1983, February). Increasing bat velocity (part 2). *Athletic Journal*, 54-55.

DeRenne, C., & Branco, D. (1986, February). Overload or underload in your on-deck preparation? *Scholastic Coach, 32*, 69.

DeVries, H.A. (1966). *Physiology of exercise for physical education and athletics*. Dubuque, IA: Brown.

Gambetta, V. (1986). *Medicine ball exercises videotape*. Lincoln, NE: National Strength & Conditioning Association.

Gambetta, V. (1986). *Plyometric training videotape*. Lincoln, NE: National Strength & Conditioning Association.

Hatfield, F. (1985, April). Power and the legs. *Sports Fitness*, 85-89, 116.

Hill, B. (panelist) (1983). Coaches roundtable: Prevention of athletic injuries through strength training and conditioning. *National Strength & Conditioning Association Journal, 5*(2), 14-19.

Jobe, F. (1990). *Shoulder and arm exercises for baseball players*. Inglewood, CA: Champion Press.

Kuznetsov, V. (1975). Speed and strength. *Soviet Sports Review, 12*(3), 78-83.

Palmeri, G.A. (1983). The principles of muscle fiber recruitment applied to strength training. *National Strength & Conditioning Association Journal, 5*, 22-24.

Robinson, C., Jensen, C.R., Sherald, J.W., & Hirschi, W.M. (1974). *Modern techniques of track and field*. Philadelphia, PA: Lea & Febiger.

Sharp, R., Troup, J., & Costill, D. (1982). Relationship between power and sprint freestyle swimming. *Medicine and Science in Sports and Exercise, 14*, 53-56.

Shellock, F.G., & Prentice, W.E. (1985). Warming-up and stretching for improved physical performance and prevention of sports-related injuries. *Sports Medicine, 2*, 267-278.

Verkhosansky, Y., & Tatyan, V. (1983). Speed-strength preparation of future champions. *Soviet Sports Review, 18*(4), 166-170.

Wimore, J.H. (1977). *Training for sport and activity*. Boston: Allyn & Bacon.

Yessis, M. (1988). *Secrets of Soviet sports fitness & training*. New York: Arbor House.

CHAPTER 5

Sports Medicine: Managing Injuries

Herb Amato
James Madison University

It's a week before the conference tournament, and you need to win the upcoming game to qualify. Your star pitcher has been out for 2 weeks due to a rotator cuff strain. His doctor told him to rest for 2 weeks, use ice, and take anti-inflammatory medication, and that is exactly what he did. His arm was feeling great during the pregame warm-up, and you made the decision to let him pitch. The first inning he looked good. He struck out one hitter and got two easy ground outs. He came into the dugout excited and feeling very good. By the fifth inning, the team had a 1-0 lead. Pitching to the third batter in that inning, your star pitcher grabbed his shoulder, and his face showed signs of pain.

Could the outcome of this scene have been more favorable to your team? This chapter will help you answer that question.

WHY SPORTS MEDICINE IS IMPORTANT

For as long as people have been participating in athletic competition, there has been a need for sports medicine. *Sports medicine* is a general term and includes any profession that works directly with the medical and health needs of the athlete. Sports medicine has become increasingly specialized, with many subdivisions. The three types of professionals most commonly associated with this field are physicians, physical therapists, and athletic trainers.

A baseball coach needs to know which of these specialists are available in his community and when to use each. Your own knowledge of sport injuries should not be the sole basis for decisions about the safety and health of your players. Whether an athlete is recruited by a major college, drafted in a high round, or continues to participate may be determined by whether he is injury free or how well he has recovered from an injury.

Baseball has changed little since its creation in Cooperstown, New York, in 1839. However, sports medicine has progressed from taping ankles and massaging cramps to a scientific specialty incorporating the knowledge and expertise of many areas. Early critics of sports-medicine workers claimed that injuries to athletes should be treated in the same ways as injuries to nonathletes. The knowledge gained through scientific research since that time has indicated that this is seldom true. The needs of athletes, and the demands they place on the injured body part once healed, are very different from those of nonathletes.

Time and rest are important to any injury. This treatment protocol alone may work very well for a nonathlete. However, you need to make sure your athletes are being treated with the goal of returning to competition, not just to everyday activities. If exercise, medication, and a wide range of therapeutic modalities will speed up recovery time and decrease the reinjury rate, these options must be considered. This alone is a major reason for sports medicine to be a part of any baseball team. As you know, an injured athlete cannot help himself improve or help his team win.

Considering that the overall health of athletes is better today and that baseball players have access to sports medicine clinics and specialists from childhood on, treatment of athletic injuries is now routine. A few decades ago their treatment was nonexistent. In 1930, there were only 128 physicians per 100,000 people, and sports medicine played a very small role in the medical world. The ratio of physicians is now higher, and many physicians are now specializing in areas that can benefit today's athletes. With the increased number of certified athletic trainers and physical therapists entering the area of sports medicine, the opportunities for the athlete to have his needs met are very good. A second opinion or an athlete's referral by a team physician to an orthopedist or a hand specialist, for example, is not uncommon. Through the use of medication, therapeutic modalities, and surgical techniques (particularly arthroscopic surgery), recovery time has been greatly reduced. Improvements in our knowledge about rehabilitation have reduced the reinjury rate. Year-round conditioning and weight training have been helpful in preventing injuries. A coach must make prevention his long-term concern and let sports medicine specialists get involved with his team. These people can help meet the team's medical needs so the coach can concentrate on the game of baseball.

This chapter takes a look at decision making for a coach. Because only about 10% of the high schools in the United States and even fewer baseball youth leagues have daily access to certified athletic trainers, the coach is the primary caretaker of the athlete's medical needs. The decisions most important to a coach and an athlete are how to determine the severity of an injury and how to treat the injury. The other questions a coach must deal with daily include when to refer an athlete to a doctor, when to take an athlete out of a game, and when to allow him to play after an injury. An emphasis on winning, or the injured athlete's desire to play again, sometimes make these decisions very difficult. Not all of these questions can be answered in this chapter, but the following information should give you a greater understanding of the important role sports medicine plays in the game of baseball.

SPORTS MEDICINE CONCERNS IN BASEBALL

A coach's responsibility includes the safety and well being of each baseball player. Areas involving first aid, secondary healing, and rehabilitation are usually under the supervision of a medical specialist. However, in the area of prevention the coach has the sole responsibility for what is to be done throughout the year.

How Do I Prevent Baseball Injuries?

The area of sports medicine that most directly benefits a baseball team is that of preventing athletic injuries. Prevention does not start 2 weeks before the season. It is a year-round process that at different times includes the five components of physical fitness—flexibility, muscle endurance, muscle strength, cardiovascular endurance, and neuromuscular coordination.

The athletic year for a baseball team can be divided into four seasons: off-season, preseason, in-season (regular season), and postseason. In each of these seasons, different demands of overall conditioning need to be placed on the players to help keep them free from injury.

Off-Season

The off-season begins about 2 weeks after the final game and lasts until the beginning of a structured preseason. The time frame for the off-season is hard to pinpoint, given the tremendous number of games in a wide variety of fall, winter, spring, and summer leagues. The off-season is not an intense time of the conditioning process. However, it is not appropriate for the baseball player to do nothing at all during this time. This time of the year is a key to preventing injuries. It is the base or foundation for the entire year. Its activities should be designed to promote endurance and flexibility.

Endurance programs are divided into two groups: muscle endurance and cardiovascular endurance. A program designed for muscle endurance and flexibility will concentrate on all major muscle groups. For greater detail on total body conditioning, see chapter 4, "Exercise Physiology: Proper Conditioning." There should also be increased emphasis on the body parts that will have added stress placed on them during the baseball season. Pitchers and hitters, for example, need additional endurance work and flexibility exercises for the throwing arm or the hand and wrist.

An athlete needs to overload the muscles to improve muscle endurance. The amount of weight will vary according to the number of sets and repetitions asked of the athlete (see Table 5.1). The general rule is that the number of repetitions must exceed 13 to increase the endurance of a muscle. Doing overload exercises two or three times a week is sufficient for developing the foundation for later muscle strength development. This progression will greatly help reduce muscle injuries. The smaller muscle groups, such as the rotator cuff muscles, wrist extensors, and wrist flexors, benefit from endurance conditioning four to six times a week (see Figures 5.1, 5.2, and 5.3). Overloading these smaller muscle groups is done by using dumbbells or hand weights of any kind (1 to 8 pounds) and surgical tubing (see Figures 5.4 through 5.13). The surgical tubing is recommended for any type of rotation exercise for the shoulder or the elbow.

Some form of isokinetic muscle training is also recommended during this season. A typical protocol for a baseball player would be to use the orthotron 2 or 3 days a week at a setting between 6 and 9. In comparing isokinetic training to conventional weight training, scientific research

Table 5.1
Weight Program

Leg curls—3 sets of 15 repetitions (starting weight 15 pounds)

Day	Sets	Repetitions	Repetitions actually performed	Weight
Monday	1	(15)	15	15 lb
	2	(15)	15	15 lb
	3	(15)	15	15 lb
Wednesday	1	(15)	15	20 lb
	2	(15)	12	20 lb
	3	(15)	8	20 lb
Friday	1	(15)	15	20 lb
	2	(15)	15	20 lb
	3	(15)	13	20 lb
Monday	1	(15)	15	20 lb
	2	(15)	15	20 lb
	3	(15)	15	20 lb
Wednesday	1	(15)	14	25 lb
	2	(15)	9	25 lb
	3	(15)	6	25 lb

Bench press—4 sets of 5 repetitions (starting weight 80 pounds)

Day	Sets	Repetitions	Repetitions actually performed	Weight
Tuesday	1	(5)	5	80 lb
	2	(5)	5	80 lb
	3	(5)	3	80 lb
	4	(5)	1	80 lb
Thursday	1	(5)	5	80 lb
	2	(5)	5	80 lb
	3	(5)	5	80 lb
	4	(5)	5	80 lb
Saturday	1	(5)	5	85 lb
	2	(5)	5	85 lb
	3	(5)	4	85 lb
	4	(5)	3	85 lb

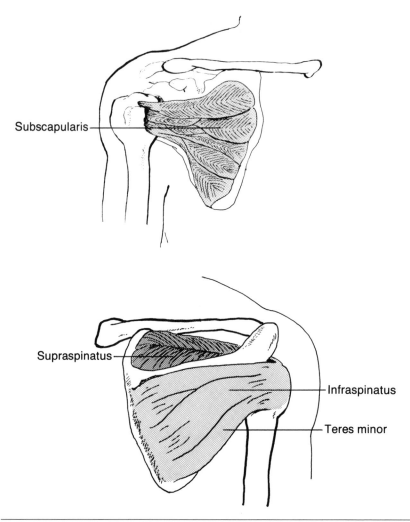

Figure 5.1   Rotator cuff muscles.

shows that weight training with standard free weights allows muscles to work at a speed between 60 and 120 degrees per second. At best, when you are trying to develop power in a nonfunctional activity, the muscle can only be worked at speeds around 180 degrees per second. High-speed cinematography of the throwing motion of a pitcher and the sprinting of a base stealer has shown that throwing-arm speed may be as fast as 300 degrees per second and the movement of the base stealer's legs may be as fast as 220 degrees per second. This information indicates that conventional weight training alone is not sufficient to develop muscle endurance and muscle strength. If isokinetic conditioning is available,

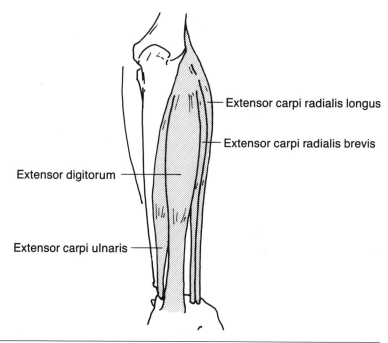

Extensor carpi radialis longus

Extensor carpi radialis brevis

Extensor digitorum

Extensor carpi ulnaris

Figure 5.2   Wrist extensors.

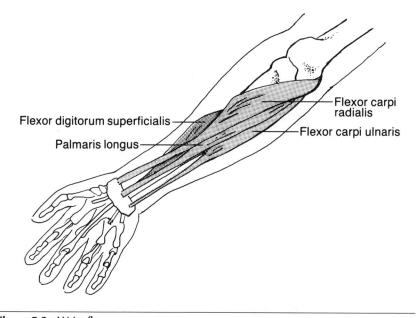

Flexor carpi radialis

Flexor digitorum superficialis

Flexor carpi ulnaris

Palmaris longus

Figure 5.3   Wrist flexors.

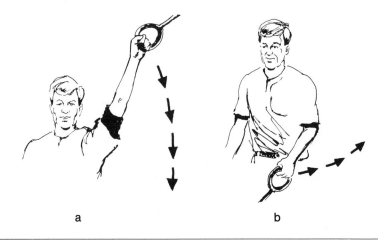

a   b

Figure 5.4   Using surgical tubing to strengthen (a) the adductors of the shoulder and (b) the abductors of the shoulder.

Figure 5.5   Using a dumbbell or weight to strengthen the abductors of the shoulder.

use it in conjunction with free weights and functional activities to improve overall muscle development.

No matter how good your off-season weight training program is, your players must do functional activities such as throwing or running to avoid injuries and wasting valuable time in the preseason. Throwing does not have to progress past short- and long-toss routines to be beneficial to injury prevention. These routines are similar to ones described in a later section, "Putting Sports Medicine to Work for You." The major difference in the progressions of the short- and long-toss routines is that now you

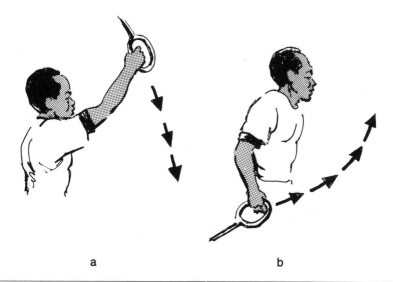

Figure 5.6   Using surgical tubing to strengthen (a) the extensors of the shoulder and (b) the flexors of the shoulder.

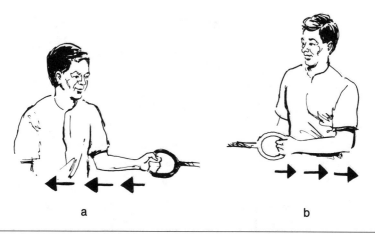

Figure 5.7   Using surgical tubing to strength (a) the inward rotators of the shoulder and (b) the outward rotators of the shoulder.

are working with a healthy athlete. To have the greatest benefits, your athletes need to throw 4 or 5 days a week between 50 and 60 throws in both the short-toss and the long-toss routines. It is important to include warm-ups in the total number of tosses in each of the routines. Because these are healthy athletes, it may be more practical for the players to throw for about 20 minutes in each of the short- and long-toss routines

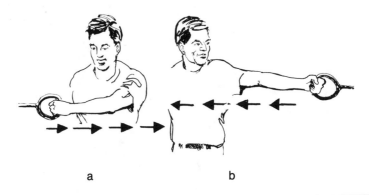

a   b

Figure 5.8   Using surgical tubing to strengthen (a) the horizontal extensors of the shoulder and (b) the horizontal flexors of the shoulder.

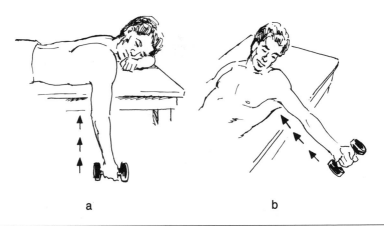

a   b

Figure 5.9   Using a dumbbell or weight to strengthen (a) the horizontal extensors of the shoulder and (b) the horizontal flexors of the shoulder.

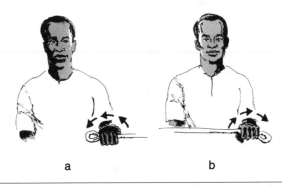

a   b

Figure 5.10   Using surgical tubing to strengthen (a) the pronators of the elbow and (b) the supinators of the elbow.

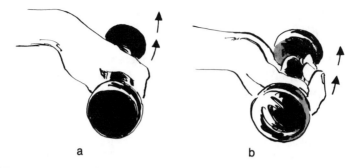

Figure 5.11 Using a dumbbell or weight to strengthen (a) the wrist extensors and (b) the wrist flexors.

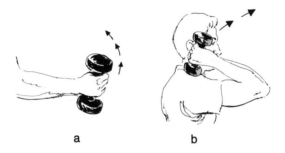

Figure 5.12 Using a dumbbell or weight to strengthen (a) the muscles that allow the wrist to do radial deviation and (b) the muscles that allow the wrist to do ulnar deviation.

Figure 5.13 Using a rubber ball or Playdough to strengthen the flexors of the hand.

rather than counting the number of tosses. Good development of the cardiovascular system should place great enough demands on the legs to have them ready for the intensity of the preseason. For greater detail, see chapter 4, "Exercise Physiology: Proper Conditioning."

Preseason

The baseball preseason takes on a much more intense and exciting atmosphere than the off-season. It would be nice to have a preseason of 6 weeks. However, it is not possible for most teams to start that far before the first game. A shorter preseason makes the off-season even more important in preventing injuries. You do not want to waste valuable preseason time on drills and exercises that could have been done by the athletes before they reported to camp. Remember that most overuse injuries occur during the preseason. A good foundation of total body fitness must be developed at some time, for the body to withstand the stresses of an entire season; if it hasn't been developed in the off-season, you must use good judgment in progressing your baseball players in the number of swings, balls thrown, and sprints allowed during the preseason.

The progression in the weight room from the off-season to the preseason should be from muscle endurance to muscle strength and muscle power. Muscle strength is developed by decreasing the number of repetitions and increasing the amount of weight (see Table 5.1). The primary difference between muscle strength and muscle power is the incorporation of a time factor with each set. It is very important to maintain a good flexibility program throughout the course of the year. The flexibility program allows your players to achieve maximum strength gains without causing muscles to shorten. Not striving to obtain good muscle balance and allowing the muscle groups to shorten are two factors that must be avoided in any conditioning program; they not only increase your player's chances of injury, but also hurt their performance on the baseball field.

In-Season

Endurance-type exercises for the hand, wrist, elbow, and rotator cuff muscles of the shoulder are important to maintain throughout preseason and in-season training. You can have your athletes continue with the exercises begun in off-season using hand weights and surgical tubing (see Figures 5.4 through 5.13).

Often during the baseball season, weight training and conditioning activities take a backseat to the game itself. Studies by the Boston Red Sox show that pitchers' shoulder strength decreases an average of 5% from the beginning of the season to the end of the season. Any time there is a reduction in strength without a reduction of stress placed on the body, the chance of injury to that body part increases. It is important to find time to maintain total body conditioning throughout the season.

Not much has been said about neuromuscular coordination, but for the healthy athlete a normal practice schedule has many interrelated activities that will improve this area. Activities that indirectly improve the interaction between the muscular and nervous systems are balance and agility drills and the development of speed and power.

Postseason

The final season is the postseason, the 2- to 3-week period following the last game. This time is used for rest and recovery. Baseball is the last thing that should be on your athletes' minds. Do not allow your athletes to assume their injuries will go away by themselves. Rehabilitation may need to start this early to ensure that the same injury does not recur.

Prevention through conditioning is important. Very few injuries in baseball occur from getting hit by a pitch or twisting an ankle while making a misstep onto second base. Baseball injuries usually occur when the body becomes tired or the muscles become weak from fatigue or there are poor muscle balance and poor flexibility from the start. By developing the five components of physical fitness throughout the year (see Table 5.2), the chance of these injuries occurring is greatly reduced.

Table 5.2
Seasonal Conditioning Program

Fitness component	Off-season	Preseason	In-season	Postseason
Flexibility	Daily	Daily	Daily	_____
Muscle endurance	2-3 days/week	_____	_____	_____
Muscle strength	_____	3 days minimum	Maintenance program	_____
Cardiovascular endurance	2 days minimum	3 days minimum	Maintenance program	_____
Neuromuscular coordination	2 days minimum	Daily	Daily	_____
Functional activities	4-5 days/weeks	Daily	Daily	_____
Rest rehabilitation	_____	_____	_____	As needed

How Do I Handle Injuries to My Players?

Because not all injuries can be prevented, treatment plans must be developed. A coach's first responsibility to an injured player is to determine the severity of the injury and decide whether to move the athlete off the playing field or wait for medical help. If moving the athlete is not a concern, then referring the athlete to a physician must always be considered. As a precaution for situations in which you may be unsure what to do, you should have a predetermined plan for emergencies (see Figure 5.14).

Any first aid given to a new injury is known as "acute care." There is very little controversy among professionals regarding recommended treatment for an acute injury. This treatment is ice, compression, and

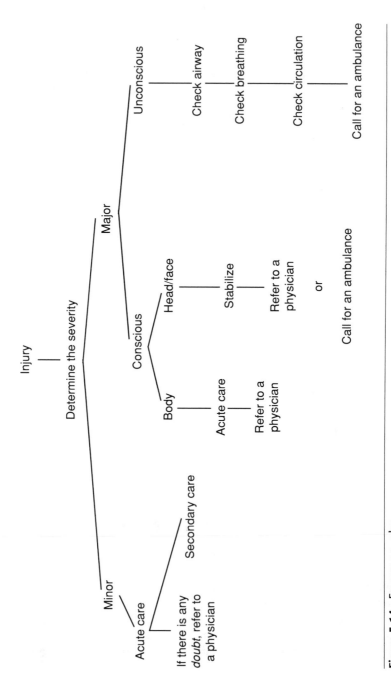

Figure 5.14 Emergency plan.

elevation. Any soft tissue injury will benefit from this treatment plan by slowing down the swelling and by preparing the area for healing to take place. Immobilization is the fourth stage of the treatment plan; however, this stage should be left up to the physician or a person trained in emergency medical care.

Any treatment beyond immediate first aid is known as "secondary care" and should be under the direction of a physician. With the exceptions of rest, basic rehabilitation principles, and functional exercises mentioned in this chapter, you should use your outside medical resources to help speed up the healing process of your athletes. There are a wide range of modalities available involving cold, heat, electricity, and sound waves. If given a chance, these resources can benefit your athlete greatly.

Ice may be the modality of choice in both acute care and secondary care. In acute and secondary care, the recommended treatment time is 20 minutes. However, the off time will vary depending on the condition of the injured area. If an injury is still showing signs of swelling and increased temperature, it needs to be treated as an acute injury. In acute care, the off time will be only 20 minutes; this decreases the amount the body warms itself, which in turn prevents increased circulation and additional swelling. In secondary care, the body is able to handle the increased circulation, and off time will be between 2 and 3 hours to allow the body to warm itself. This warming is accomplished by the body reflexively increasing the amount of blood to the injured area. This additional blood brings needed oxygen, nutrients, and white blood cells to aid in the healing process.

What Are the Most Common Injuries Experienced by Pitchers?

This section discusses only injuries to the shoulder and elbow. These injuries are the most common due to overuse by pitchers. Shoulders and elbows are not, however, the only areas injured by pitchers. Use common sense and the helpful hints from the next section of this chapter in the treatment of the rest of the body. Any time you are not sure of the medical condition of your athlete, refer him to a physician.

Medial Epicondylitis (Little League Elbow)

This is a common injury to any player who does a lot of throwing. This condition is an inflammation of the muscles that attach to the inside of the elbow (see Figure 5.3). The amount of swelling and pain will be proportional to the number of muscle fibers involved. The arm movements that will be most affected are flexing the wrist and turning the lower arm in an inward direction. This condition should be treated using the guidelines of secondary care.

Rotator Cuff Strains

Rotator cuff muscles help hold the upper arm and shoulder blade (see Figure 5.1). A great deal of force is exerted on these muscles during the acceleration and deceleration phases of the throwing motion. With repeated trauma, microtears begin to develop in the muscle fibers. This tearing and overstretching is referred to as a "strain." If not treated, these small tears may lead to a complete rupture of the muscle or muscle tendon. A complete tear of one of the rotator cuff muscles will cause sudden pain and a loss of power. It may also give the athlete problems while resting or doing everyday arm movements. The amount of pain and discomfort with a strain is proportional to the amount of tearing and overstretching. This condition should be treated using the guidelines of secondary care.

Rotator Cuff Tendinitis

This condition is an inflammation of one or more of the rotator cuff muscle tendons (see Figure 5.1). The pain will be located around the glenohumeral joint with some referred pain down as low as the distal end of the deltoid muscle. This pain usually gets worse during activity and subsides with rest. The rotator cuff muscles play an important role in all phases of the throwing motion, which makes it difficult to distinguish which phase is causing the most pain. This type of tendinitis is hard to distinguish from subdeltoid and subacromial bursitis, due to the similarities. In many cases the bursas and tendons are both inflamed from overuse. This condition should be treated using the guidelines of secondary care.

Subdeltoids and Subacromial Bursitis

These two conditions are very similar in nature, with pain and tenderness just under the acromion process. The athlete will experience most of his pain with these conditions during the acceleration phase of the throwing motion. Bursitis-type injuries are usually from overuse or poor throwing mechanics and should be treated under the general guidelines of secondary care, with corrections of the throwing motion during the functional exercises.

What Are the Most Common Injuries Experienced by Other Baseball Players?

Baseball players will have a variety of injuries ranging from simple bruises to severe head injuries. Coaches must be prepared to handle the first aid of all injuries and know when to refer to a physician. Overuse injuries of the throwing arm can be treated in about the same manner as a pitcher's arm. Injuries mentioned in this section are primarily related to acute conditions.

Baseball Finger (Mallet Finger)

This condition involves a piece of bone being pulled away by the extensor tendon from the main part of the distal phalanx of the finger. In this injury, the athlete's chief complaint will be his inability to bring his distal phalanx into extension. The two primary causes for this type of injury are the finger being hit by a baseball or the finger being forced into extreme flexion. Other injuries with similar mechanisms would be fractures or dislocations of the bones of the hand and fingers. In all cases, the treatment should be under the supervision of a physician.

Contusion (Bruise)

This type of injury can occur anywhere on the body in baseball. However, contusions are usually associated with muscles that have been hit by a ball or from a collision with another player. A hitter may experience a bruise to the hands from the bat. In most cases, contusions are minor injuries. The amount of tissue damage and swelling will be proportional to the amount of force that caused the injury. The plan of action for this type of injury will fall under the guidelines for acute care. The coach must always be ready for this type of injury to the head or face. This injury can be serious, and the predetermined plan for an emergency may need to be carried out to meet the athlete's needs.

Lateral Epicondylitis (Tennis Elbow)

This problem usually occurs when a player has been taking a great deal of batting practice. The pain and swelling will be located on the outside of the elbow (see Figure 5.2). The movements that will most aggravate the elbow are extension of the wrist and turning the elbow in an outward direction. The elbow most often affected during hitting is the one nearest the pitcher. This overuse injury benefits from using the guidelines for secondary care.

Ligament Sprains

The function of a ligament is to connect a bone to another bone that gives stability to a joint. A sprain is overstretching or tearing of a ligament. Sprains are not very common in baseball. Occasionally the ligaments to the ankle and wrist, hand, or fingers are affected. Acute care is important in the recovery time for this injury. If there is any doubt about the severity, you should have a physician decide the treatment plan.

Muscle Strains

This type of injury can happen to any muscle. It is an overstretching or disruption of muscle fibers. It can be as minor as a microtear of relatively few muscle fibers to a complete rupture of many fibers. The severity of a muscle strain is proportional to the amount of swelling, diffused tenderness, muscle spasm, and observed protection of the muscle when the athlete is asked to actively move the body part. The care given here should be consistent with general acute care and basic rehabilitation principles.

Navicular Fracture

This injury may occur from overuse; however, the primary mechanism of injury is falling on an outstretched hand. The pain and point tenderness are located at the base of the thumb. The movement causing the most pain would be grabbing the bat or squeezing a ball. This injury needs to be treated by a physician.

What Are the Early Warning Signs of Injury?

Communication among the baseball player, coach, and athletic trainer is essential to prevent minor injuries from becoming major problems. Players must not try to hide an injury or mask the pain with medication. You must make clear to them the importance of reporting all injuries. When pain is allowed to continue over an extended period, a cycle develops that leads to muscle disuse, weakness, and atrophy. Pain is a sign that something is wrong, and the injured body part should be evaluated by a physician or an athletic trainer.

The most common visual warning sign for the lower extremities is limping as the player walks or runs. The hitter or pitcher may be favoring a particular body part during the batting swing or pitching motion. If problems of this type are not treated, they may lead to other injuries involving the throwing arm or hip and back.

Among the warning signs for the upper extremities (particularly the throwing arm), the arm and its relationship to the shoulder are primary. In general, you are looking for any type of form change in body mechanics. These changes may involve the entire body with regard to coordination of the upper and lower body and the rotation of the trunk and hips. The key to using early warning signs is to know the normal throwing motion for each of your players. The indicators that need to be observed most are any changes in the height to which the player elevates his arm and the amount of posterior movement of the arm during the cocking phase. If the arm is having problems due to injury or fatigue, the player will compensate by dropping the arm from its normal position or not bringing it back as far as normal. If this happens, it may look as if the pitcher is pushing the ball rather than throwing it to home plate. Another problem a pitcher will have is in his follow-through. If a pitcher lands flat-footed or on the heel of his lead leg, this is a good sign that he is in trouble. A good follow-through is usually a positive sign that the other phases in the throwing motion were done correctly.

Changes in form and delivery will be easier to notice in the pitcher than in other players on the field. Pitchers control the beginning and starting position of each pitch. In contrast, the other fielders, including the catcher, are often throwing off-balance and from different locations on the field. Watch for any changes in the fielder's and catcher's deliveries during routine plays or a structured warm-up period.

The warning signs that most often indicate that a player is having trouble can be observed by watching the baseball. First, look for any reduction in the velocity of the ball. Second, if there is a decrease in the velocity, the pitcher will usually have less movement on the ball, and the rotation on the ball will not be as tight. For a position player, the ball may be taking more bounces to a specific base than usual. Third, the location of the ball will tend to be high in all players. The communication between the catcher or first baseman and the coach is valuable in determining when the pitcher and infielders begin to lose control of the ball. In the pitcher's case, the catcher has the best perspective on what the baseball is actually doing for each pitch. The catcher normally picks up on a pitcher's problem before the coach does. This communication among players and the coach is a major step in preventing injuries.

What Basic Rehabilitation Principles Apply to Baseball Injuries?

In most cases, the goal in any rehabilitation program is to return the athlete to his preinjury level of fitness in the least amount of time. If the prior fitness level of the injured body part was the cause of the injury, then the goal of the rehabilitation program must be to surpass the previous fitness level to prevent the injury from recurring. Any overuse type of injury is usually caused by muscle weakness. In these cases, preinjury muscle strength was not great enough for the demands being placed on the body part. In some cases, the overuse problem is related to poor body mechanics. It is hoped that you can make the proper adjustments in mechanics before the problem develops into a serious injury.

Basic rehabilitation principles are very similar to weight lifting principles. Both sets of principles are based on progression and overload. The primary difference is that in rehabilitation, you are dealing with a specific body part. Using nonfunctional exercises and functional activities, you must also design the program specifically for the position your athlete plays. Nonfunctional activities are designed to develop the five components of physical fitness under controlled situations. For the most part, a nonfunctional exercise is any exercise performed in the weight room. These activities are not sports-related; however, the demands placed on the body part during competition must be considered. Functional activities are very much sport-related. These exercises deal primarily with running, throwing, catching, and hitting. If you understand the injured body part and the demands of playing a particular position on the baseball field, you will be able to devise a rehabilitation program that meets the needs of your injured athlete.

Rehabilitation Guidelines

There are certain guidelines for rehabilitation programs that, if followed, increase the likelihood of a healthy and speedy recovery. Probably the most important guideline in administering a rehabilitation program is using the absence of pain and swelling as your keys for progressing to the next stage of the rehabilitation program. Many times in this chapter it is noted that if there is pain or swelling during or after the workout, you must regress the demands being placed on the injured athlete. Pain and swelling are the body's way of saying, "This is too much work." Due to the effects of gravity, it is difficult to see swelling on the shoulder. Joint tightness may at times work as this guideline. You and your athletes need to understand that trying to work through pain and swelling will lead to more problems. If your athlete pushes too hard, the added problems he produces will prohibit him from progressing at a normal rate.

Within the limits of the absence of pain and swelling, you must push your athlete to work as hard as possible. Muscle strength and muscle endurance are very important in the overall rehabilitation program. The guideline of muscle development cannot be overlooked and can only be developed by overloading the muscle. This is done by gradually placing a greater stress on the muscle or muscle group, and the simplest method is by increasing weight in nonfunctional exercises such as a leg curl on the universal machine or the bench press using free weights. In Table 5.1, the principle of progressive overload is used in both the leg curl and the bench press. By reviewing Table 5.1, you can see that the athlete was asked to do three sets of 15 repetitions (3 x 15 repetitions) using 15 pounds on the leg curl machine. Once the athlete can do what is asked of him, he can increase the weight by 5 pounds. By increasing the weight to 20 pounds on Wednesday and keeping the sets and repetitions the same, you have developed an exercise using the progressive overload principle. The early part of the rehabilitation program is trial and error. To help prevent reinjury, it is much better to start with a light weight and progress to a heavier weight. If the weight you choose first was so light that the athlete could easily lift the 3 x 15 repetitions, or if the athlete could only do 8 repetitions in the second set and 3 repetitions in the third set, you know that you need to adjust the amount of weight used in each set. The progressive overload principle can be applied to any exercise. In the weight room, remember that the simplest way to overload a muscle is to add weight once the athlete does the number of sets and repetitions that were asked of him.

Progressive overload in functional activities is not an objective. Examples of functional activities in baseball are catching, throwing, hitting, and running. Running and throwing are discussed later in this chapter. However, any time you are overloading a muscle, you must increase the amount of stress placed on it. These added demands in functional activities will vary from player to player, depending on playing position and whether the player is healthy or recovering from an injury.

The third guideline in a rehabilitation program is that all activities are designed to show a progression. This chapter has discussed the proper progression dealing with muscle endurance and muscle strength. However, the development of range of motion, power, and proprioception must be designed with progression as a key factor.

The proper progression in any rehabilitation must include both nonfunctional exercises and functional activities. Nonfunctional exercises progress through five stages—range of motion, muscle endurance, muscle strength, power, and proprioception. Range of motion is the movement within a given joint. Muscle endurance is the ability of a muscle or muscle group to sustain effort over a prolonged period; it is developed by working muscles against light resistance through many repetitions. Muscle strength is the ability of a muscle or muscle group to do a maximum amount of work for a very short time period or for one lift in the weight room. Muscle strength is developed by working muscles against heavy resistance and low repetitions (3 × 5 repetitions). Power is the amount of work done in a unit of time (power = work/time). To develop power in a rehabilitation program, a time element must be incorporated into the exercise. This is done by asking your athlete to, for example, swing a baseball bat as hard as he can for 20 seconds or to do as many tricep curls as he can in 30 seconds using a 15-pound weight. The final stage in the nonfunctional progression is the development of proprioception. These specialized sensory receptors relay messages pertaining to body position back to the brain. After an injury, the body's proprioceptors must be reeducated to allow the body part to know its location in space. Think about running down a gravel road and your foot landing on a rock. You react quickly by moving the leg so that the ankle is not injured. That type of movement or reaction is proprioception. You must redevelop it after an injury to ensure a safe return for your athlete. Any types of balancing exercises or jumping on uneven surfaces will work to develop proprioceptors.

The final two guidelines in developing a solid rehabilitation program are designing it so that it has a great deal of positive reinforcement and ensuring that the athlete understands what is going on in the program. Positive reinforcement can be provided by verbal commands and improvement. The verbal reinforcement is often overlooked. It is hard to encourage one injured athlete when you are trying to prepare the rest of the team for the next game. Rehabilitation can become very boring, and it is easy for an athlete to slack off if there is no formal supervision. This alone may slow down the athlete's progress and keep him out of the lineup for a longer time than necessary. The best way to show improvement is to increase the amount of weight in small increments during your progressive overload exercises. By doing this, the athlete will be completing the task asked of him at a greater frequency. This allows him to increase weight every few days instead of every few weeks. For the player to understand what is going on in the rehabilitation program, you must have good communication with the physician, the parents, and the athlete. You must be honest with the athlete about his injury. Rehabilitation is a day-by-day progression. Telling an athlete he will be ready to play in 2 weeks, for example, is not a good idea. He will expect to play on that day. In his mind, you have lied to him if he is not ready to perform. This could be a major stumbling block for his motivational level. Be honest with your injured athletes, and make the rehabilitation process a day-by-day progression.

PUTTING SPORTS MEDICINE TO WORK FOR YOU

The following case studies indicate how you can properly use sports medicine to rehabilitate your players. These two scenarios describe specific injuries. However, you will need to adapt these upper and lower extremity functional routines to your athletes' injuries and positions. The demands on a catcher are very different from those outlined in the two scenarios. You must first look at the injured body part and design functional activities to meet the needs of the injury. Progression and patience are very important components of these functional routines. Do not get carried away with taping the injured body part. You must allow the body part to recover and progress without the use of tape. Taping should occur only when the athlete starts in game-situation activities, when you know the muscles and ligaments are providing support and not the tape. Absence of pain and swelling lets you know that the workout has been within normal limits; however, never having swelling or pain may mean the athlete is not working hard enough. This could also slow down recovery. The road to recovery is a fine line; you need to push as much as possible, but pushing too hard will also slow down the recovery.

Case Study: Proper Rehabilitation
of an Injured Throwing Arm

As was the case in the scenario at the beginning of this chapter, rotator cuff tears often happen after periods of rest. The rotator cuff consists of four muscles: supraspinatus, infraspinatus, teres minor, and subscapularis (see Figure 5.1). These muscles are no different from any other muscle—they atrophy and weaken with inactivity. If an athlete has been casted and on crutches for 2 weeks, do not even consider letting him play the day after the cast is removed. The same goes for an athlete whose arm has been totally restricted in its activity, even if it has not been in a cast.

You must gradually increase the arm's activity level and use absence of pain and swelling or joint tightness as a guide during the athlete's recovery. With any strain, not just rotator cuff injury, ice and gentle range of motion exercises are very important. The decision to use anti-inflammatory medication should be made by the athlete's physician. Once easy range of motion exercises can be performed without pain, the functional progression should begin (Figure 5.15). Because this injury involves the throwing arm, one must design the rehabilitation program specifically for the individual and his position on the baseball field. Have a pitcher start with mirror throwing, using his normal windup and also throwing from a stretch, and starting in the stance phase before every pitch. You will want him to go through the entire throwing motion, but each phase of the motion should be done slowly and correctly. This is called a "mirror" phase because the athlete is being either observed by himself (in a mirror) or his coach or monitored with a video camera. If no pain or swelling or joint tightness persists with the mirror throwing, the athlete should progress to using a baseball and to a 1-pound weight or a weighted baseball to continue this phase.

There is a fine line between overworking an injured body part and not working the body part hard enough. Overworking may reinjure the body part, and this slows down the progress. However, not working the injured part hard enough delays the progress and prevents the athlete from competing. With mirror throwing, repetition is very important, but use pain and swelling or joint tightness as the guide to avoid crossing the line to reinjury.

Progressing to the short-toss routine (the next stage of the upper extremity progression) does not mean that mirror throwing has to stop. The continuation of mirror throwing keeps the pitcher thinking of good form and proper body mechanics.

The short-toss routine should start with athletes at 20 feet apart. To ensure that the injured pitcher does not toss too vigorously, do not allow his partner to wear a baseball glove. If there is pain at 20 feet, the athlete

Day	Upper extremity — Nonfunctional activities	Upper extremity — Functional activities	Lower extremity — Functional activities	Lower extremity — Nonfunctional activities
1	Range of motion	Range of motion	Range of motion	Range of motion
2	Range of motion	Mirror throwing	Range of motion	Range of motion
3	Range of motion	Mirror throwing	Range of motion	Range of motion
4	Muscle endurance	Short toss	Controlled weight-bearing	Muscle endurance
5	Muscle endurance	Short toss	Controlled weight-bearing	Muscle endurance
6	Muscle endurance	Long toss	Controlled weight-bearing	Muscle endurance
7	Muscle endurance	Long toss	Heel raises	Muscle endurance
8	Muscle strength	Long toss	Heel raises	Muscle strength
9	Muscle strength	Long toss	Walking	Muscle strength
10	Muscle strength	Form pitching	Running	Muscle strength
11	Muscle strength	Form pitching	Running	Muscle strength
12	Power	Form pitching	Running	Muscle strength
13	Power	Form pitching	Running	Muscle strength
14	Proprioception	Form pitching	Running	Power
15	Proprioception	Game day	Game situation	Power
16	Proprioception	Short toss	Game situation	Proprioception
17	Proprioception	Long toss	Game situation	Proprioception
18	Proprioception	Form pitching	Game day	Proprioception
19	Proprioception	Game day	Continue rehabilitation	Proprioception

* Modifications should be made according to the absence of pain and swelling
* There will be overlap between activities

Figure 5.15   Rehabilitation of a baseball injury.

is not ready for the short-toss routine. Move back to the mirror phase only and continue to work range of motion and nonfunctional activities. The proper progression in this phase is to increase the amount of time the pitcher is allowed to throw each day, and as time increases you may also want to increase the distance between the pitcher and catcher up to 30 feet. When the time reaches 20 minutes or 60 throws of the short-toss routine per day at 30 feet, the athlete is ready to progress to the next phase of the functional activity. The major concern once again is pain-free activity and the absence of swelling or joint tightness in the shoulder area the next day.

The next phase is the long-toss routine. Your injured pitcher stands near the outfield foul line, and his partner stands in straightaway center field. The keys to this phase are for the ball to have a good arc on it and the pitcher to use good body mechanics. The progression in this phase starts with the pitcher throwing the ball a little over half way and just hard enough that it will roll to his partner. If this cannot be done without pain, the pitcher must regress to mirror throwing and short-toss. As pain-free movement allows, the injured athlete increases the throwing distance. Eventually the ball will be arriving to his partner on two bounces, then one bounce, and then in the air with a good arc. This should be continued until the injured partner can throw for about 20 minutes or 60 throws in this long-toss routine. The distance of the long-toss routine should never exceed 150 feet. Do not hesitate to back the pitcher off this long-toss routine if he is starting to have arm pain or is using improper body mechanics. Each day the athlete is in the long-toss routine, use mirror throwing and the short-toss routine as a warm-up. Before having the athlete throw the first ball, have him break into a sweat by doing some type of running activity. Sweating is a good indicator that the body is warmed up and ready for more strenuous activity.

In the long-toss routine, do not let the pitcher start throwing the entire distance to his partner on the first throw, even if on the preceding day he was able to finish by throwing the entire distance. Start each long-toss routine by progressing the throws from hitting the ground halfway in front of the partner so the ball rolls to him, to bouncing it right in front of the partner, to throwing so that the ball can be caught in the air. These throws should be counted as part of the 60 long-toss throws each day. This progression keeps the pitcher from throwing too hard too soon. When the pitcher can painlessly complete the long-toss progression, he is ready for the fourth step of the functional throwing progression—form pitching.

After a good warm-up of the long and short-toss routines, the pitcher takes the pitching mound. He starts at half speed, if pain allows, and progresses to full velocity over the next several days. Keep in mind that you must watch for good form and no noticeable compensation for the previous injury. Do not allow the pitcher to throw anything but fastballs until he has reached maximum velocity. Ideally, a radar gun is needed to compare his speed now with the records of his fastballs in previous games. If a radar gun is not available, watch the movement and the tightness of the baseball's rotation. Also observe the follow-through and the height of the ball when released. These four factors can give valuable information on the velocity of the baseball.

In the beginning of form pitching, keep the number of pitches to 25 per day. Once maximum velocity with the fastball has been reached, progress to a change-up and then to breaking pitches. Do not rush into breaking pitches. It may be several days between throwing the change-up to throwing a curveball without pain. Too much time and energy has been invested in this athlete to speed up this segment of the functional progression. However, the pitcher must be able to throw all of his pitches comfortably during practice. Once this happens, the day everyone has been waiting for is here—game day.

The remaining setback is that game day is still part of the rehabilitation process. Pregame warm-up may take a major toll on your pitcher. He may throw as many pitches in warm-up as he has thrown in any 1 day of practice. Record the velocity of his pitches (if possible) during warm-up and decide at that time whether he is ready to pitch. If your decision is to let him pitch, then count pitches in the entire game, not just innings. Remove him from the game at the first sign of trouble. This may seem very conservative, but in his first outing remove him from the game after 25 to 35 pitches.

The total number of pitches with pregame warm-up, pre-inning warm-up, and game pitches will probably exceed 60 pitches. Pain and swelling or joint tightness once again are your keys to determining whether the athlete is recovering as you have hoped he would after this amount of time. With throwing only 25 to 35 pitches in the game, the pitcher should have a quick recovery. He probably will be able to pitch on 3 days of rest (4-day rotation).

The decision of when the pitcher will be ready for his second start is not based on time alone. You must watch his recovery the next 3 days, observing the short-toss routine, long-toss routine, and form pitching. Short-toss or gentle throwing is recommended for most players the day after the game. If there are no signs of reinjury to the arm, this easy throwing motion will help increase blood flow, which benefits recovery time by removing waste products from the shoulder area. Following the short-toss routine on the first day, the next day should consist of the long-toss routine. The third day is followed by form pitching. In the second outing, the number of game pitches will be increased to 50 to 65. If you detect any problems (visually or with the radar gun), you will have to remove him sooner. There is no magic to this functional progression, just common sense and the use of pain and swelling or joint tightness as your guides.

Case Study: Proper Rehabilitation of an Injury to a Lower Extremity

Upper extremity injuries are not the only injuries you will see in the game of baseball. In this next scenario, we have an outfielder sliding into second base. Once the dust has settled, you discover that he has injured his ankle. The first stage of the recovery process begins with good acute care. The best way to judge the severity of the injury is with X-rays and a physician's evaluation. Much of the early recovery process is based on the physician's recommendations.

Once the initial healing has occurred, it is time to start the injured athlete on a lower extremity functional routine (see Figure 5.15). This routine must be a slow and gradual process. Pain and swelling are the two key factors determining whether the athlete is working too hard. Start with easy range of motion exercises with the injured ankle, consisting of up-and-down movements of the foot, and then progress to writing the alphabet in the air and in cold water with the injured ankle.

The next stage toward recovery is controlled weight-bearing. This may be done with the use of a cane or crutches. In the beginning of this stage, you will need good communication with your team physician. The athlete now starts heel-raise exercises. He stands at the side of a table with the injured side nearest the table, then lifts both heels off the floor, putting only as much body weight on the injured ankle as pain-free movement allows. The hand nearest the table can be used for balance and for taking weight off the injured ankle. Remember not to hesitate to regress to the earlier stage if pain does not allow the athlete to perform the exercise. The progression in this stage is to place more weight on the injured body part until the athlete can perform the exercise with no support from either the uninjured leg or the hand nearest the table. The number of sets and repetitions depend on the amount of pain and swelling the athlete is experiencing. This exercise is designed to develop muscle endurance and to some degree work range of motion. As mentioned earlier, research shows that a minimum of 13 repetitions are needed to develop muscle endurance. However, the athlete may not be able to do this number at the beginning, which is why slow progress is important to meet the needs of the injured athlete. The number of sets should be increased daily if the athlete is not having any problems. Do not put a limit on the number of sets in a day. If the athlete did 18 sets yesterday but today he is showing signs of discomfort, you know that this number of sets was too many. When the injured ankle has had enough work, it will start showing signs of swelling and pain. Stop at this point and use the immediate-care treatment of ice, compression, and elevation.

There will be overlap between stages in all sections of this functional routine. Keep this in mind each day by observing the beginning segments of the next stage in the lower extremity functional progression. You do not want the injured athlete to stay in only one stage when he may be able to start the next step of the progression.

The next stage in the functional routine is walking without a limp. This stage may start days before the athlete is able to complete heel raises without support from his hand or uninvolved leg. Walking is another exercise on which no limits need to be placed, unless the athlete starts limping. If he does, he may be placed back on crutches or even required to stay off the injured leg. Keeping this injured outfielder from moving around is not always an easy chore, but limping is a sign that something is wrong. If you allowed him to continue walking, his progress would be impeded and he would be kept in the dugout for a longer time than needed.

The next stage of the lower extremity functional routine is running. The injured outfielder runs straight ahead on even surfaces at half speed, going the distance between home plate and first base. The proper progression is to gradually increase speed and distance. Once the athlete can run straight ahead with no pain, he can start making a wide turn and continue toward second base. Do not allow your athlete to land on first base or to make a sharp cut toward second base, both of which could lead to reinjury. Any time the outfielder feels he is comfortable with throwing, allow him to start with a short-toss routine. Observe his ability to push off the injured foot and his ability to land on it. Do the same with hitting, starting with the batter hitting tossed balls and progressing slowly to live pitching. The next step in the running progression is to gradually increase the speed and amount of running the outfielder is allowed to do each day. Jogging backward in a straight line on even surfaces is the next step. If no pain or swelling persists at the time of running or the next day, allow your athlete to increase the speed and distance of this phase.

If the outfield is grass and the infield sand, it is time to move the athlete to the uneven grass surface. Repeat the earlier steps of the running routine. The injured ankle may have trouble making the adjustment from the smooth infield to the rough outfield, but once this adjustment has been made it is time for the athlete to start changing speeds. Have him run at a slow pace and move to a faster pace and back to a slower pace. Incorporating starting and stopping in this phase will prepare the athlete to progress to more difficult baseball activities.

As throwing and hitting activities continue to improve, you must place greater demands on the outfielder's injured ankle. This is done by side-to-side running in both directions, running figure eights (progressing from large eights to smaller eights) and cutting movements in forward and backward directions.

The final stage in the functional running routine includes situations the athlete may face in a game. The outfielder's position requires that the athlete be able to go in all directions to catch fly or ground balls. You should have the athlete simulate these movements first without the ball and then have him catch the ball in practice situations. Progress the outfielder from just catching the ball to catching the ball and throwing it to different bases. He must also be placed in situations at the plate and on the bases that he may see later in game situations. It is much better to find out in practice that he cannot do an activity. This gives him the opportunity to stop without reinjuring the ankle. Examples of these activities are hitting the ball and running toward first base, hitting the ball and cutting on first base toward second base, and leading off first base and breaking toward second base. Once the outfielder can handle any situation you place him in, it is time to put him back in the lineup.

KEYS TO SUCCESS

- **Prevention needs to be a year-round concern. Without it you are leaving the health and welfare of your team to chance.**
- **Many times the team with the fewest key injuries is the team that wins the most games.**
- **The more time spent with exercises designed to help prevent injuries, the less time you will need to spend with acute care, secondary care, and rehabilitation activities.**
- **Communication among the coach, the injured player, and the sports medicine community can help meet the demanding and changing needs of the baseball world.**

RESOURCES

Andrews, J., McCluskey, G., & McLeod, W. (1976). Musculo-tendinous injuries of the shoulder and elbow in the athlete. *Athletic Training,* **11**(2), 68-71, 74.

Bertman, S. (1988). *Short and long toss routine.* Unpublished team material, head baseball coach, Louisiana State University, Baton Rouge.

Cicoria, A., & McCue, F. (1988). Throwing injuries of the shoulder. *Virginia Medical,* **115**(7), 327-330.

Costell, D. (1977). Science and the future of sports. *Physician and Sportsmedicine,* **5**(6), 102.

Croce, P. (1987). *The baseball player's guide to sports medicine.* Champaign, IL: Leisure Press.

Culpepper, M. (1985). Sports medicine and sports science: Bridging the gap. *Alabama Medicine*, **55**(5), 47-49, 51.

Francis, A. (1984). Sports science and the coach. *Scottish Journal of Physical Education*, **12**(2), 41-46.

Heatwole, R.L. (1989). *Starting pitchers: Pre game warm-up routine*. Unpublished team material, head baseball coach, James Madison University, Harrisonburg, VA.

Hinton, R. (1988). Isokinetic evaluation of shoulder rotational strength in high school baseball pitchers. *The American Journal of Sports Medicine*, **16**(3), 274-279.

Kurucz, R. (1976). *Prowess*. Unpublished manuscript, West Virginia University, Morgantown.

Jobe, F., & Bradley, J. (1988). Rotator cuff injuries in baseball prevention and rehabilitation. *Sports Medicine*, **6**, 378-387.

Jobe, F., & Nuber, G. (1986). Throwing injuries of the elbow. *Clinical Sports Medicine*, **5**(4), 621-636.

Pappas, A.M., Zawacki, R.M., & McCarthy, C.F. (1985). Rehabilitation of the pitching shoulder. *American Journal of Sports Medicine*, **13**(4), 223-235.

Shapira, W. (1975). Injuries and responsibilities. *Physician and Sportsmedicine*, **3**(2), 34.

Smith, N., & Stanitski, C. (1987). *Sports medicine: A practical guide*. Philadelphia: Saunders.

Zarins, B., Andrews, J., & Carson, W., Jr. (Eds.) (1985). *Injuries to the throwing arm*. Philadelphia: Saunders.

CHAPTER 6

Nutrition: The Winning Diet

Gale Beliveau Carey
University of New Hampshire

Jim and Neil aren't brothers, but they should be. Since grade school they've played together, mowed lawns together, gone to the beach together, and studied together. They even look alike—tall, lanky, glasses, brown hair, and full of energy. Now they're both starters on the high school varsity baseball team. Jim's at first base; Neil's in center field.

The season started out great, and by midseason the team had an 8-1 record. But about that time, Jim and Neil began to look less alike. Both were still lanky, wore glasses, and had brown hair, but their energy levels were very different. Neil stopped running laps with Jim before practice. He wanted to but just couldn't—admitting he had no energy. Shagging flies was OK, but when it came to an all-out sprint after a line drive, Neil felt like he was moving in slow motion. His legs were heavy, his breathing was labored. Frustrated, Neil couldn't figure out why he felt so tired, so lifeless. After all, he and Jim slept the same amount and studied the same amount, and both played ball. Laughing to himself, he thought of the only difference between them, one that he teased Jim about. Jim brings his lunch to school every day and must be home for dinner by 6:30 or heads roll. Neil eats lunch in the cafeteria and has fast-food dinners several nights a week because his parents often work late. Surely this couldn't make a difference. Or could it?

It could. Neil's poor food choices at the cafeteria and his fast-food dinners may have caught up with him. Improper nutrition is a sure-fire way to invite fatigue, something any athlete wants to avoid.

Getting the best performance from your players is only possible with good nutrition. As a coach, you can make this happen. You can put the information you learn from this chapter into practice. By learning some concepts of the science of nutrition, you can advise your players not only on what to eat, but on why they should eat as you say. Explaining why carries you over the threshold from being a disciplinarian to being a wise coach.

The place to start is to educate yourself. The second step is to educate your players. The third step is to watch your players practice and perform at their healthiest and best.

WHY NUTRITION IS IMPORTANT

For athletes, good nutrition is critical. Baseball players put a lot of stress on their bodies, demanding that their arms throw harder and legs run faster. The energy drained out must be put back, and the only way to do that is by eating properly.

To the body, food means energy. It also means structure. From infancy to adulthood, our bodies process food and turn it into one of two things: structure or energy. The body makes an eyelid, or stores energy to blink that eyelid. It makes muscle, or it gathers energy to contract that muscle. Food is how we grow. You really are what you eat.

Food turned into structure is easy to see—bones, muscles, hair. Good nutrition is essential for building structure. But what about food turned into energy? Food energy is fats and carbohydrates. Food also includes vitamins and minerals, which don't provide energy themselves but help release energy from fats and carbohydrates to the body. Food turned into energy is less visible than food turned into structure. That is, of course, unless you get too much food—pot bellies are very visible.

Carbohydrates are critical for ballplayers. Why? Because hard-working muscles love to burn carbohydrates for energy. The harder a muscle works, the more carbohydrates it will burn.

What happens when the muscle runs out of carbohydrate? The muscle will still function, but only at half speed because now it has only fat to burn. Marathoners who run out of carbohydrate, or "hit the wall," must slow down and walk. A similar thing happens to ballplayers. Swinging the bat becomes harder, and running down a line drive takes twice the normal effort simply because their muscles have run out of carbohydrate.

The carbohydrate stored in muscle is called "glycogen." To see how important glycogen is to an athlete, take a look at Figure 6.1.

The figure shows two things: (a) The more carbohydrates in the diet, the more glycogen in the muscle, and (b) the more glycogen in the muscle, the longer an athlete can exercise before becoming exhausted. Simply put, the more carbohydrates an athlete eats, the more endurance he has.

The practical side to all of this is that muscle glycogen can be formed only by eating food carbohydrates. If there are not enough carbohydrates in the diet, muscle glycogen levels drop.

What other factors contribute to good nutrition? Water is essential for keeping the body cool. If the body overheats, it slows down. With adequate carbohydrates and water, the right balance of vitamins and minerals, and a moderate supply of protein, your players will be on the road

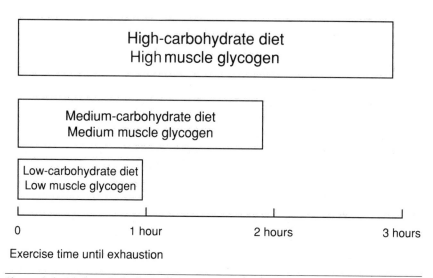

Figure 6.1 High-carbohydrate diet: more muscle glycogen = more endurance. *Note.* From "Diet, Muscle Glycogen and Physical Performance" by J. Bergstrom, L. Hermansen, E. Hultman, and B. Saltin, 1967, *Acta Physiologica Scandinavica,* **71,** pp. 144-145. Adapted by permission.

to good nutrition and, because of it, peak performance. A star pitcher suffering from poor nutrition can still pitch, but his fastball may arrive home at 82 miles per hour instead of 87. A quick shortstop suffering from poor nutrition may miss those grounders in the hole that he would normally reach.

NUTRITIONAL CONCERNS IN BASEBALL

Nutrition, as it applies to baseball, can help your team. Here are some questions that you, as a coach, may want answered:

What is the best playing weight?

How can my players maintain high energy levels and good concentration during practices and games?

Do catchers and pitchers have different nutritional needs than outfielders?

What should my players eat before, between, and after games?

Are nutritional supplements helpful?

What Is the Best Playing Weight?

Ballplayers are always aware of their body weights, whether they admit it or not. An extra 3 pounds of fat can mean diving for a line drive but missing it because they are too slow. How much should your players weigh? Are you aware of your players' body weights and their weight goals? Do you bring up the subject of weight with them only if they need to lose? We'll look at recommended body-weight ranges for baseball players and what factors can influence these ranges.

How Can My Players Maintain High Energy Levels and Good Concentration During Practices and Games?

Energy is measured as calories. Calories, which are in food mainly as carbohydrates, fats, and proteins, can be burned (during exercise) or stored (after eating). And not all food calories are identical. That is, the body handles carbohydrate calories differently from fat or protein calories. It's carbohydrate calories that are critical for the athlete.

By eating high-carbohydrate diets, your players will still be strong going into the 11th inning in game two of a doubleheader. We'll look at why carbohydrates are important and how your players should eat to ensure they get enough.

Another important nutrient for keeping energy levels up is water. As the body's coolant, water has everything to do with performance. The heat your players generate, or the heat they absorb standing in center field on an 85-degree day, needs to be gotten rid of. Water is what carries the heat away. The heat is captured by sweat, and the sweat releases this heat back into the air as vapor. If the body keeps "vaporizing" its water but doesn't have a fresh supply of water coming in, it becomes overheated—a dangerous condition.

Do Catchers and Pitchers Have Different Nutritional Needs Than Outfielders?

Of all the defensive positions, catchers and pitchers are the ones who are moving the most. Does this extra energy expenditure affect their nutritional needs, compared to an outfielder who may only field seven balls during a whole game? Probably not. As long as these players are getting sufficient calories and, more importantly, the right kind of calories, their nutritional needs should be met.

What Should My Players Eat Before, Between, and After Games?

How soon a player eats before game time can have a big impact on his performance. In general, the closer to game time an athlete eats, the fewer nutrients get to his muscles. This is partly because of hormones released by the body and partly because the blood, which carries oxygen and nutrients, swarms to the intestines to help absorb the nutrients just eaten. Because blood can't be in two places at once, the muscles get less blood. If the player has just eaten, the muscles suffer and may actually be starving for nutrients when the first pitch is thrown.

Just as important as when to eat is what to eat. We'll take a look at what foods are good to eat before a game and when they should be eaten.

It's important to replenish energy stores with the right kind of calories after a game, too. Most school budgets are tight these days, so they might support only a fast-food postgame meal. We'll look at how healthy food choices can be made even when eating fast food.

Are Nutritional Supplements Helpful?

Today athletes are looking for an edge, that extra something that will help them throw harder and run faster. Can nutritional supplements provide this edge?

Nutritional supplements can range from a single nutrient to a whole army of nutrients or even a meal. These nutrients are the same ones found in food. Many of them are required by the body. Their names are enough to boggle the mind. *Pantothenic acid. Molybdenum. Selenium.* These things sound like components of a nuclear bomb. How much do we need of these nutrients? Wouldn't it be good insurance to take a supplement?

Not necessarily. For one thing, nutritional scientists really aren't certain how much of some of these nutrients the body needs. For another, scientists also say there may be nutrients the body needs that they aren't aware of yet. Keep in mind that Mother Nature gives us our nutrients in food. She's designed both the food and the body, intending the food to meet the body's needs. So getting nutrients from food is the best way to ensure that the body is getting what and how much it needs. Eating a variety of wholesome foods ensures the body is being fueled properly. The more variety, the better the likelihood that the body is getting what it needs. And the more wholesome the food, the better the likelihood that nutrients haven't been removed during processing. Eating a variety of foods provides nutritional balance. We'll take a look at how easy it is to follow a sound nutrition plan based on variety.

There may be instances when supplements are needed, and we'll look at these instances. Supplements won't buzz a healthy pitcher's fastball up from 80 to 90 miles per hour, but they may improve an unhealthy center fielder's leg speed.

So sit back, relax, and read on for some nutrition knowledge. The rest of this chapter touches on these concerns plus gives you some tips on how to be a nutritionally aware coach.

PUTTING NUTRITION TO WORK FOR YOU

A major challenge for you as a coach is to put words into action. Diagraming a 3-6-3 double play is one thing, but it takes getting onto the field and moving through the play, again and again, to make it stick. The same goes for nutritional knowledge. You could tell your athletes to read this chapter. Better, though, is to show them. This section is designed to help you do just that.

What Are the Keys to Good Nutrition?

Good nutrition can play a major role in the success of a competitive baseball team. What is good nutrition? Everyone has his or her own ideas. Some think it means eating your vegetables, others think it means avoiding snacks, still others think it means taking a vitamin pill every day.

Good nutrition means eating foods that provide the body with the necessary balance of vitamins, minerals, energy, and water it needs, every day. Sounds simple enough, but putting this into practice, especially in today's world of convenience foods and fast-food eating, is a challenge.

For the athlete, good nutrition is critical. Baseball players are really endurance athletes—they are either playing or practicing for 2 or 3 hours a day, running and throwing, using the same muscles day after day. The energy used up must be restored, and the only way to do this is through good nutrition. The key components to good nutrition for athletes—carbohydrates, water, and variety and balance in the diet—together provide athletes with the energy and nutrients needed for peak performance.

Heavier on the Carbohydrates, Lighter on the Fats

Carbohydrates are one of the three macronutrients in foods. The others are fats and proteins. *Macro* simply means big; macronutrients are nutrients present in large amounts in food. It's from the macronutrients that the body gets its energy.

Macronutrients in food = Fat + Carbohydrate + Protein = *Energy*

Micronutrients, on the other hand, are vitamins and minerals. These are needed by the body in much smaller quantities than the macronutrients. But don't be fooled—a smaller requirement doesn't mean less important! Vitamins and minerals are critical to the body. They provide no energy to the body by themselves but help extract energy out of the macronutrients.

The body needs all three macronutrients—fat, carbohydrate, and protein—because each serves a different function. Food protein provides the building blocks for body protein—muscles, hair, nails, digestive juices. Food fat provides energy for the body and chemicals essential for making hormones. And food carbohydrate keeps blood sugar levels normal and provides muscles with quick energy. It is this quick energy that is so important to baseball players.

The best diet for a baseball player is one that has 60% of calories coming from carbohydrates, 15% of calories from protein, and 25% of calories from fats. Teaching your athletes how to achieve such a diet is one goal of this chapter. More on this later.

                FOOD   BODY
Protein ——————————> muscles, hair, nails, digestive juices

Fat ——————————————> hormones, energy

Carbohydrate ——————> blood sugar, muscle carbohydrate,
                     quick energy

Carbohydrates

Because carbohydrates are good energy for the body, you might think that your ballplayers should eat plenty of carbohydrates the night before a big game. This is only partly true. The whole truth is that your players should eat plenty of carbohydrates all during the competitive season.

To see why, let's go back in time. Several years ago, a group of healthy men, ages 22 to 34, were asked to participate in an experiment at Ball State University in Muncie, Indiana. They were asked to run for 2 hours every day while eating a normal diet. Muscle glycogen levels were measured before and after the run each day. Then they were switched to a high carbohydrate diet, and the same muscle glycogen measurements were made.

The results were amazing! Take a look at Figure 6.2 and notice that when the subjects ate the normal diet, they were gradually drained of muscle glycogen. In fact, by Day 3, several said they couldn't run, they felt so tired. On the other hand, when they ate the high-carbohydrate diet, they replenished their muscle glycogen each day, despite a taxing workout. They also felt great!

Your ballplayers are just like these men, because daily practices of sprinting, throwing, hitting, and sliding deplete muscle glycogen. The only way for your players to replenish the glycogen is by eating carbohydrates. Later in the chapter we'll look at sample menus that show how easy this is to do.

Protein

How much protein do baseball players need? We used to think, "Muscle is made of protein, so an athlete who's working his muscles needs to eat a lot of protein." And so eating steak and eggs before the big game became a ritual.

Now we know better. We understand that, yes, muscle is made of protein, but, no, it doesn't burn protein for its energy. It burns carbohydrate and fat.

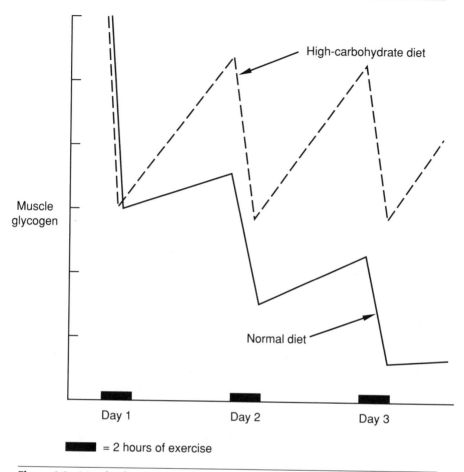

Day 1

Day 2

Day 3

= 2 hours of exercise

Figure 6.2   Muscle glycogen must be restored daily by eating a high-carbohydrate diet. *Note.* From ''Nutrition for Endurance Sport: Carbohydrate and Fluid Balance'' by D.L. Costill and J.M. Miller, 1980, *International Journal of Sports Medicine,* **1**, p. 4. Adapted by permission.

Then why does an athlete need protein? First, it helps form new muscle in an athlete who is still growing. Second, it replaces those proteins in a full-sized athlete that have been destroyed as part of normal life processes.

How much protein is enough? For a growing teenager or young adult, the protein from 5 to 8 ounces of meat plus three to four glasses of milk each day is sufficient. This equals a turkey sandwich of 2 to 4 ounces of meat at lunch, a 1/4-pound hamburger at dinner, and three to four glasses of milk each day. Eating more protein than this doesn't cause the body to make more muscle: The only way an athlete adds muscle to his body is through hard, physical work and good, balanced nutrition.

Fats

Without fat in our food, eating could be very dull. Let's face it—who looks forward to eating a salad without dressing, a chunk of homemade bread without butter, or a pizza without cheese? Without a doubt, fats add flavor to food. They also satisfy our appetites, provide us with calories, and contain nutrients essential for our health.

One thing about fats, though, is that they do pack a punch. One ounce of fat has more than twice the calories of one ounce of carbohydrate or protein. Because fats can make food so tantalizing, it's easy to overconsume many of the fat-containing foods. Active athletes may argue that they won't retain those extra calories because their energy is being burned off, and that is probably true. But the problem is not the number of calories, it's the fact that for each calorie of fat taken in, one fewer calorie of carbohydrate is consumed. Only carbohydrates can replenish muscle glycogen stores. So carbohydrates should get first priority in the diet and fats should follow.

Variety and Balance

Two key components of good nutrition are variety and balance. There is no such thing as a perfect food—a food that has the proper balance of all essential nutrients. Given that the body requires many nutrients, some of which are still being discovered, how do we get what we need?

The best way to get the proper balance of vitamins, minerals, and other essential nutrients is by offering the body a wide variety of foods. It can then pick and choose the nutrients it needs.

Variety means choosing different foods from each of the six food groups, as often as possible. By subdividing the traditional four food groups into six, nutritionists hope to ensure that we get plenty of food variety. What are the six food groups? They are meat and meat alternatives, milk, grain and other (see p. 166), fruit, vegetable, and fat. Getting variety within the vegetable group, for example, doesn't mean eating cream-style corn one day, canned corn the next, and corn-on-the-cob the next. It means eating corn one day, broccoli the next, and carrots the next. Each of these vegetables has a different nutritional strength. Carrots are high in vitamin A; corn is high in carbohydrates; and broccoli is high in vitamin C.

Remember that carbohydrates are especially important for the athlete's diet. A diet rich in high-carbohydrate foods will provide high energy. Of the six food groups, three are sources of carbohydrates. The three are the grain (and other), fruit, and vegetable groups. These should be emphasized in the athlete's diet.

In today's busy world, it is easy to get into "food ruts"—eating the same foods day after day. Many people do this at breakfast, eating cereal, milk, orange juice, and toast every day. By simply varying the kind of cereal, the kind of toast, the topping for the toast, and by eating differently on weekends, they can break the rut. Although this can be challenging for young adults on the go, simply making them aware of the importance of variety in the diet may help them change their habits.

What about balance in the diet? A balanced diet means eating daily from each of the six food groups. Let's take a closer look at these groups.

The six food groups are:
Meat and meat alternatives
Milk
Grain and other
Fruit
Vegetable
Fat

Meat and Meat Alternatives.   Meats and meat alternatives are good protein sources. This group includes animal products such as beef, chicken, turkey, eggs, and fish and nonanimal products such as beans, peanut butter, and tofu. By choosing from the meat group, the athlete gets good-quality protein to keep his muscles healthy.

Meat and meat alternatives includes beef, chicken, eggs, fish, and lunch meats. But it also includes peanut butter, beans, and tofu.

A little bit of meat goes a long way. Americans tend to eat much more meat than they need—for your average-sized athletes, about 6 ounces a day should be sufficient. Larger players will need a bit more. Some meats are high in fat, so learning which meats are lean can be a healthy advantage.

Vegetarians also need protein, and theirs will come from nonanimal products. Nonanimal proteins are lower in quality than animal proteins. Eating grains (bread, pasta, etc.) or drinking milk along with nonanimal proteins can boost the quality of the protein. Advise your vegetarian players to be sure they get enough servings from the meat food group and always eat grain-based food or drink milk along with these servings. And remind them that their nonanimal proteins must be eaten at the same time as the milk or carbohydrate, or the boosting effect is lost. Also, remind strict vegetarians who avoid all animal products to take a vitamin B_{12} supplement and be sure to get sufficient iron and calcium.

Milk.   Milk also provides good protein. The milk group includes cheese, yogurt, ice cream, and ice milk in addition to skim or low-fat milk. Like the meat group, some milk foods have a lot of fat, especially ice cream and whole milk. For your players who are lactose intolerant (unable to digest milk products), there are low-lactose milk products on supermarket shelves now; otherwise, the possibility of taking calcium supplements should be explored with a family physician.

Milk includes cheese, yogurt, and ice cream as well as whole, low-fat, and skim milk.

Grain and Other.   The grain and other group includes high-carbohydrate foods, and these are the cornerstone of a healthy diet for your players. High-carbohydrate foods include bread, cereals (hot and cold, except granola), pasta, pancakes, waffles, muffins, and other grain products. Vegetables such as potatoes and corn are also high-carbohydrate foods that for the purpose of a balanced diet, can be considered along with this group. The carbohydrates in all of these foods are complex (also called "starch"), meaning that the molecules are connected like a strand of pearls. The other kind, simple carbohydrates (also called "sugars"), are molecules that are not attached to each other. They are found in table sugar, maple syrup, honey, and most cookies and candies. These foods have little nutritional value. The healthiest diet is one in which most carbohydrates are complex.

Grain and other includes breads, cereals, spaghetti, pancakes, waffles, potatoes, and even corn!

Fruit.   Both types of carbohydrates are also found in fruits as sugar or starch. Fruits such as apples, oranges, bananas, and pears are all good sources of fiber, vitamins, and minerals. Fruit juices and jams are also members of this group. Beware, though, that many "fruit juices" contain very little fruit and are mostly corn syrup. Advise your players to read the ingredient list on the juice container, remembering that the first item listed is present in the largest amount, the second item is present in the second largest amount, and so forth. If you want a real fruit juice, look for one with the fruit, not corn syrup, listed first or second on the ingredient list.

Fruit includes fruit juices and jams as well as typical items like apples, oranges, bananas, and pears.

If you want a real fruit juice, look for one with fruit, not corn syrup, listed first or second on the ingredient list.

Vegetable.   Vegetables also provide complex and simple carbohydrates and make up another group that is a good source of fiber, vitamins, and minerals. This group includes broccoli, carrots, celery, tomatoes, green beans, lettuce, and even V-8 juice. Salad bars are a good spot to load up on vegetables, and raw vegetables are good snack foods.

Vegetable includes carrots, celery, broccoli, tomatoes, green beans—even V-8 juice!

Fat. The last group is fats. Food items in this group include nuts, seeds, salad dressing, butter, margarine, and alcohol. Fat also sneaks into the meat and milk groups as well as most prepackaged foods. People who eat a lot of cheese, salad dressings, and regular cuts of meat are eating a high-fat diet. Small amounts of certain types of fat are essential, but too much fat can be harmful. High-fat diets are thought to increase the risk of heart disease, diabetes, and even some types of cancer. The more calories an athlete eats as fat, the fewer he will eat as carbohydrate, and the less quick energy he will have.

Fat is found in nuts, seeds, salad dressings, and butter. It is also hidden in many convenience foods like potato chips and certain crackers, packaged desserts, frozen dinners, and microwave items.

The Supplement Story

Athletes today want a competitive edge, and many athletes hope that supplements will provide it. Health food stores, drug stores, even local supermarkets have shelves loaded with vitamins, minerals, amino acids, lecithin, bee pollen, and sterols. Muscle magazines have advertisements that promise greater strength to readers who buy their special supplements.

Over 40% of high school and college athletes believe these ads and take supplements regularly, thinking supplements will improve their health and performance. Do supplements really help? No, they don't. There is no proven benefit to taking supplements as long as an athlete is eating a balanced, nutritious diet.

One coach recently asked, "But aren't supplements good insurance, especially on days when you don't eat right?" Sure, taking a multivitamin-mineral pill will do no harm. For some, it may be a psychological boost. But taking megadoses of one or a few nutrients can be harmful, as certain nutrients are toxic at high levels (vitamin A, for example). Also, large doses of nutrients can upset the body's balance of other nutrients. Either way, there is no substitute for Mother Nature, or good nutrition.

So what should you tell your athletes? Tell them that many scientific studies have tried to show a performance boost from supplements but have failed to show it. Tell them the bottom line: Unless an athlete is deficient in a nutrient, adding extra nutrients to an already adequate diet does absolutely nothing. Tell them that eating right is the best thing they can do for themselves.

Getting Enough Water

A truly forgotten nutrient is water. About 60% of the human body is water. Water transports nutrients, oxygen, and carbon dioxide to and from the body tissues. It also lubricates joints. And most important, it maintains normal body temperature.

As the body's coolant, water has everything to do with performance. The heat your players generate needs to be gotten rid of. Water is what carries the heat away. Swinging the bat generates heat in the muscles, blood carries this heat to the skin surface, and sweat releases this heat into the air as vapor. Poof, the heat disappears. If the body keeps "poofing" its water without a fresh supply of water coming in, it becomes overheated. Just like an overheated car, an overheated body will wear down and eventually stop.

The body can sweat out a tremendous amount of water, trying to keep itself cool. A hard-working athlete can lose 8 pounds of water in 1 hour! Normally sweat is released onto the skin surface, where it evaporates into the air, carrying the heat with it. But on a humid day the air can be so full of moisture that the sweat cannot evaporate, and it rolls off the skin. The body is unable to cool itself properly on these days, and it also loses a lot of water.

In fact, exercising in hot weather can increase the body's need for water to 5 or 6 times its normal need. Once dehydration occurs, the body's mechanism for cooling itself is broken. As you know, this can be life threatening.

What can be done? Drink, drink, drink. Cool water is absorbed faster than water at room temperature, so have cool water (refrigerator temperature) available for your athletes, if possible. It is important to impress upon your athletes the need to take in water all day long. Tell them to drink at least 8 cups of water a day. When the weather gets hot and humid, tell them to drink until they're visiting the bathroom frequently. Tell them that they should never rely on thirst alone to tell them when to drink. By the time an athlete is thirsty, it is usually too late: He should have had water 30 minutes earlier.

What about electrolyte replacement drinks? Under normal conditions, these really aren't necessary. As long as your players are eating a good, balanced diet, they will replenish lost electrolytes through their normal diet. One glass of orange juice alone replaces all the electrolytes lost in 3 quarts of sweat. But many players like the idea of drinking these fancy drinks, so let them. At least they are drinking. The most important thing is that they are getting water.

Now that we've seen the key components to good nutrition, what should your ballplayers eat?

Is There an Ideal Training Diet for Ballplayers?

The ideal training diet for baseball players is high in carbohydrate, low in fat, and moderate in protein. What does this mean in terms of food groups?

What to Aim for

Table 6.1 shows how many servings the average baseball player should be eating per day from each of the six food groups. It assumes that the average high school male weighs 150 to 170 pounds and needs at least 3,200 calories every day.

Table 6.1
Food Group Servings for Baseball Players*

Meat	Milk	Fruit	Vegetable	Grain	Fat
6	4	8	5	9	11

*Assuming players are male and body weight is 150 to 170 pounds.

How to Achieve It

How does this translate into breakfast, lunch, and dinner? Table 6.2 shows a sample menu that meets these food-group needs for a typical player.

These athletes are eating plenty of carbohydrate, going light on the fat, and getting enough protein. And most importantly, muscle glycogen levels are being kept high, which means plenty of muscle energy for quick sprinting and hard hitting.

Special Nutritional Needs

Up until now, good nutrition has been described in terms of food groups, food balance, and food variety. But there are specific nutrients that young athletes may be missing.

Surveys tell us that male athletes could be low in three nutrients: folate, iron, and calcium. Folate is a vitamin found in fruits and vegetables, two

Table 6.2
How Food Group Servings Translate Into Meals

	Meat	Milk	Fruit	Vegetable	Grain	Fat
Breakfast:						
1 1/2 cups of Cheerios					1	
1 cup 2% milk		1				1
1 large banana			1			
12 oz. glass of orange juice			2			
2 pieces of toast with jam			1/2		1	
Lunch:						
3 oz. tuna on	3					
whole wheat bread					1	
with lettuce and tomato				<1/4		
1 1/2 cups coleslaw and 1 large						
dill pickle				2		
12 potato chips						2
1 pear			1			
1 cup 2% milk		1				1
Snack:						
2 cinnamon-raisin bagels					2	
2 cups lemonade			2			
Dinner:						
3 oz. chicken breast	3					
2 cups rice					2	
2 cups steamed broccoli and						
carrots with 2 tsp margarine				2		2
Small salad with				1		
1 tablespoon Italian dressing						2
1 cup 2% milk		1				1
3 cups strawberries			2			
Snack:						
6 fig bars					2	1
1 cup 2% milk		1				1
Totals:	6	4	8 1/2	5	9	11

food groups that young, active people often skip. Many teenage boys are iron deficient, especially athletic ones. And because soft drinks have replaced milk at mealtime, young men are not getting enough calcium.

How can you advise your players so that they won't be deficient in these nutrients? Tell them

- to eat from the six food groups, including fruits and vegetables;
- to eat red meats and iron-enriched cereals and breads; and
- to drink milk at each meal and with a snack (4 cups per day).

What Body Weight Is Best?

Baseball players do monitor their body weights. A player may not like his number, but he knows what it is; and often, he wishes it was different. Americans are obsessed with weight and spend lots of dollars trying to change it.

The Ideal Body Weight

What should your players weigh to perform at their best? If they are too heavy, their running will be slow. If too light, their swings may be weak. Only the player can determine his best playing weight. Realistically, there is no magical number that each player must or should weigh. But there are some general body-weight guidelines for young adults, ages 18 to 25, as shown in Table 6.3.

Table 6.3
Body-Weight Guidelines for Male Baseball Players Ages 18 to 25

Height		Weight
(feet	inches)	(pounds)
5	2	108-132
5	3	113-137
5	4	117-143
5	5	122-148
5	6	126-154
5	7	131-159
5	8	135-165
5	9	140-170
5	10	144-176
5	11	149-181
6	0	153-187
6	1	158-192
6	2	162-198
6	3	167-203
6	4	171-209

Remember, these are general guidelines for your athletes. Besides sex and height, genetics play a big role in determining an athlete's body weight. And so does the amount of muscle versus fat. For example, a 5-foot, 6-inch athlete at 170 pounds is overweight by the standards in the table. But if he is only 8% fat, far less than the average of 15%, then his weight is mostly muscle, not extra fat. So before advising your "overweight" players to lose weight, have them get a body-fat measurement done by a trained exercise specialist. Your local sports medicine clinic should provide this service; but be sure a knowledgeable specialist is doing the measurement, as tiny errors in measurement can make big differences in the percent body fat.

Try to inquire of your players, individually, about their health and their weight. Not only will this prove you are interested in them, but you'll get information from them directly, rather than second or third hand. If a player seems dissatisfied with his weight, ask why, and what his weight goal is.

If a player wants to change his weight, and the weight goal seems realistic to you, you can help by advising him with the following information.

Losing or Gaining Safely

It's natural for people to want immediate results, especially when it comes to body weight. The first thing you need to do is impress upon the athlete that any weight change should be gradual to be effective. This goes for gaining as well as losing. If the weight loss is too rapid, it is mostly water. If the weight gain is too fast, it may be mostly fat.

The athlete who wants to lose weight should primarily lose fat. And the one wanting to gain should add on mostly muscle. How?

For the athlete who wants to lose weight, ask him to monitor for 1 week how many servings he is eating from each of the six food groups every day. Give him a copy of the chart in Table 6.4 and a copy of the food

Table 6.4
Guide for Losing Weight

Day	Meat	Milk	Fruit	Vegetable	Grain	Fat
Monday						
Tuesday						
Wednesday						
Thursday						
Friday						
Saturday						
Sunday						
Weekly totals:						
Weekly totals ÷ 7 (daily totals)						
Subtract these for weight loss:					−2	−3
New daily totals:						

group descriptions in Table 6.5. At the end of 1 week, sit down with him and his chart and work through the calculations outlined on the chart:

1. Total the number of servings from each group for the week, and divide each by seven. This will give you the average daily servings from each food group.
2. Next, subtract three servings of fat and two servings of grain from the average daily servings. This will remove about 400 calories from his normal intake and will give him new daily totals to shoot for.

Have the athlete continue to record daily food servings but now target his new goals each day. Meeting these new goals will put him on his way to losing about 1 pound a week.

To the player who wants to gain weight, give a copy of the chart in Table 6.6 and the food group description in Table 6.5. Follow the calculations outlined on the chart:

1. Total the number of servings from each group, and divide each by seven. This gives the average daily servings from each group.
2. Next, add one meat, two grains, and two fats to his totals. This will add 400 calories per day and provide him with new goals to shoot

Table 6.5
The Six Food Groups

Meat
  1 ounce lean beef, chicken, turkey
  1 to 2 ounces fish
  1/2 cup green beans
  10 medium shrimp
  1 large egg
  High-fat meats
    1 ounce bologna, salami, liverwurst
    2 strips bacon
    1 ounce sausage
    1 tablespoon peanut butter
Milk
  1 cup skim or 2% milk
  1 ounce mozzarella, Parmesan, or ricotta cheese
  1 cup low-fat yogurt
  1/4 cup low-fat cottage cheese
  High-fat milks
    1 ounce American, cheddar, Swiss cheese
    1 cup ice cream or ice milk
    1 cup hot chocolate

(Cont.)

Table 6.5
(Continued)

Fruit
  1 apple, banana, grapefruit, orange, pear
  3 tablespoons raisins
  1/2 cantaloupe
  40 grapes
  1-1/2 cups strawberries
  1/2 to 1 cup fruit juice
  Jams and jellies

Vegetable
  1 carrot, green pepper, tomato, cucumber
  1 cup string beans, zucchini, mushrooms
  1 cup cauliflower, cabbage, rhubarb
  1/2 cup broccoli, onions, squash, V-8 juice
  Unlimited lettuce

Grain
  2 pieces bread—wheat, white, rye, raisin
  1 to 2 cups cereal
  1 hamburger bun
  1 cup oatmeal, cooked
  3 medium pancakes
  1 cup plain rice, spaghetti, noodles, cooked
  1 cup corn
  1 large baked potato
  6 cups unbuttered popcorn
  2 large pretzels
  1/2 cup sherbet
  20 animal crackers
  14 saltines

Fat
  1 teaspoon butter, margarine, mayonnaise, oil
  1 tablespoon cream cheese, heavy cream, sour cream
  1 teaspoon thousand island or roquefort dressing
  2 teaspoons French or Italian dressing
  5-10 walnuts, peanuts, cashews, almonds
  2 tablespoons sunflower seeds
  1 small wedge of avocado

for. Meeting these new goals should allow him to gain about 1 pound per week.

In either case, the athlete will be achieving his goal of weight gain or loss while still eating a balanced diet.

Table 6.6
Guide for Gaining Weight

Day	Meat	Milk	Fruit	Vegetable	Grain	Fat
Monday						
Tuesday						
Wednesday						
Thursday						
Friday						
Saturday						
Sunday						
Weekly totals:						
Weekly totals ÷ 7 (daily totals)						
Add these for weight gain:	+1				+2	+2
New daily totals:						

The importance of approaching your players about their weights and health can't be emphasized enough. Listening to your players will clue you in on issues that may severely affect health and performance. Eating disorders, although much more common in women, do occur in men and can have devastating health effects.

How Should My Players Eat on Game Day?

You've prepared your team, physically and mentally. You've practiced the fundamentals over and over—sacrifice bunts, double plays, hitting the cutoff man. You've decided on your starting pitchers. You've educated your players about the best training diet. You've come this far—you certainly don't want to lose all that hard work.

Before the Game

You could lose all your hard work if your players don't eat right on game day. Take a look at some of the dos and don'ts for game-day eating in Table 6.7.

If a player eats a big meal too close to game time, blood that should be supplying muscles with oxygen and nutrients will be busy absorbing nutrients from the intestine. Consequently, the muscles suffer. Also, eating too many simple carbohydrates stimulates the fast release of insulin. Insulin is the key that unlocks cell doors and allows the simple carbohydrates to get in. That sounds good—after all, we said that muscle cells

Table 6.7
Dos and Don'ts for Game-Day Eating

The Dos
Eat the pregame meal at least 3 to 4 hours before game time.
Good pregame meals include
   Sandwiches (easy on the filling!)
   Pancakes
   Fruit
   Pasta
Eat something familiar—this is not the time to experiment!
Drink plenty of water, especially if it's hot and humid.

The Don'ts
Don't eat heavy foods at the pregame meal (e.g., meats, gravies, sauces, and
   cheese).
Don't drink soft drinks the hour before game time.
Don't play hungry—hunger pains are distracting!
Don't eat candy bars, cookies, or sugary foods within 1 hour of game time. If
   hunger strikes, eat fruit, crackers, or pretzels.

like to burn carbohydrates. The problem is that with a fast release of insulin, sugar rushes into cells, leaving little behind in the bloodstream. Low blood sugar causes light-headedness, weakness, and a slightly foggy mind—not good qualities for a baseball player starting a game!

Remember, too, that fats and proteins slow down digestion, so it's best to keep these to a minimum. This goes for pregame as well as between-game eating. The last section of this chapter has some suggested pregame meals.

During and Between Games

The dos and don'ts for pregame eating also apply to between-game eating. Snack-type foods will prevent hunger if the wait is not too long, say less than 2 hours. However, if tournament play calls for a longer wait, 3 hours or more, then a high-carbohydrate meal may be in order.

Snacking in the dugout during the game really isn't advised. Aside from stimulating digestion and diverting blood flow away from muscles, it also diverts attention away from the game. Better to encourage your players to eat a good meal several hours before the game and forget about food until after the game.

Drinking, though, is another story. Do encourage your players to drink water between and during games, especially on hot days. Have your players avoid soft drinks—they present the same problems as dugout snacking.

After the Game

After a game, your players should eat exactly as they have been during training—high-carbohydrate foods to replenish those glycogen stores. Fast-food chains are the usual spots to stop after a game, and unfortunately fast foods are high in fat and protein and low in carbohydrate. There are some exceptions, though, and the end of the chapter contains a healthy fast-food eating guide. Instead of the usual fast-food-chain stop, suggest a stop at a breakfast or pizza chain. Pancakes, French toast, waffles, and pizza all make fine high-carbohydrate meals.

What Are Some Practical Ways to Educate My Players About Nutrition?

You'll need to pass along some basic nutrition information to your athletes to lay the groundwork for healthy eating. One way to do this is by talking to them with some visual aids. Here are outlines for two short talks, 15 to 20 minutes each, that you can give before practice.

TALK #1:

Your goals:
1. To explain where food energy comes from and how the body uses it
2. To emphasize the importance of muscle glycogen to your athletes

You'll need:
A blackboard and chalk

Your approach:
1. Although you're not a nutrition expert, explain to your team that you do know that nutrition is important. All hard work goes down the drain if proper foods aren't eaten.
2. Ask your athletes why they need food (answer: for energy). Ask them where the energy comes from (answer: fats, carbohydrates, proteins; *not* vitamins and minerals).
3. Outline the food sources of fat, carbohydrate, and protein. Explain that when these foods are eaten, the body converts them into stores of fat, carbohydrate, and protein (see Figure 6.3). Explain that too much of any nutrient is converted into fat.
4. Explain that exercise uses fat and glycogen for energy, but that glycogen is the key. The harder the exercise, the more glycogen gets used up and must be replaced by food carbohydrates. If it isn't replaced, fatigue sets in. Draw the glycogen graph on the blackboard (see Figure 6.4).

Your blackboard should look like this:

then like this:

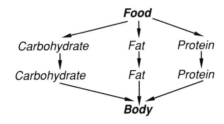

and lastly like this:

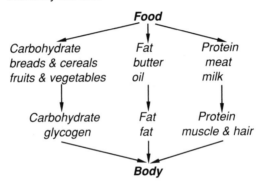

Figure 6.3   Outlining the food sources of fat, carbohydrate, and protein on your chalkboard.

TALK #2

Your goals:

1. To reinforce major points from Talk #1
2. To describe foods that are high in carbohydrate
3. To explain balanced eating from the six food groups

You'll need:

1. A blackboard and chalk
2. A can of V-8 juice, a bottle of salad dressing, a carton of yogurt, a jar of peanut butter, a bagel, a donut

Your approach:

1. Review Talk #1 by asking your players where food energy comes from (answer: fat, carbohydrate, and protein). Ask what happens to

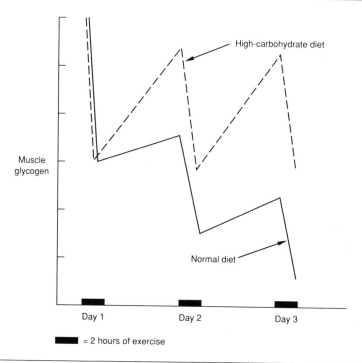

High-carbohydrate diet

Muscle
glycogen

Normal diet

Day 1   Day 2   Day 3

▬▬ = 2 hours of exercise

Figure 6.4   The glycogen graph you can draw on your chalkboard.

it in the body (answer: fat is stored as fat, carbohydrate is stored as glycogen, protein builds muscle, hair, etc.; everything can be stored as fat if too much is eaten). Ask why athletes need plenty of carbohy-drates (answer: to keep muscle glycogen stores filled; glycogen is essential for high energy).

2. Ask them to name some foods that have carbohydrate (answer: breads, cereals, bagels, spaghetti, macaroni, rice, potatoes, corn, bananas, raisins).

3. Ask about the rest of the diet. Introduce the idea of six food groups, and write them on the board.

4. On your blackboard, write that a 150-pound man needs at least nine servings from the grain group (complex carbohydrates) per day.

5. Fill in the other food groups—they should get at least five servings of fruits and vegetables, three to four milk servings, and 5 to 6 ounces of meat per day.

6. Remind them that foods like donuts and candy bars have a lot of fat. This is OK, but suggest they sometimes reach for a bagel, a piece of fruit, or some toast and jelly instead (these are carbohydrates).

7. Ask your players to guess which categories the foods you've brought with you fall into: V-8 juice (vegetable); salad dressing (fat); yogurt

(milk and fat); peanut butter (meat and fat); bagel (grain); donut (grain and fat).

8. Tell them you'll provide them with a nutrition checklist (in the following section) and can discuss guidelines for changing their body weights if they so desire (see previous section).

9. Send them off with a strong reminder to eat their carbohydrates, and give them copies of the sample menus in Table 6.8.

Table 6.8
Sample Menus for 1 Week

| | Monday | | |
Breakfast	Lunch	Dinner	Snack
Cereal, banana	Spaghetti with	Meat loaf	2% milk
2% milk	meatballs	Carrots and peas	Popcorn,
Toast and jam	French bread	Potato with yogurt	unbuttered
Orange juice	Green beans	Salad	Lemonade
	Fruit cocktail	2% milk	
	2% milk	Apple pie	

| | Tuesday | | |
Breakfast	Lunch	Dinner	Snack
Oatmeal with	Chili	Chicken breast	Cinnamon bagel
raisins	Rolls	Rice	2% milk
Toast and jam	Corn	Steamed broccoli	
Orange juice	Apple crisp	Whole wheat bread	
2% milk	2% milk	Strawberries	
		2% milk	

| | Wednesday | | |
Breakfast	Lunch	Dinner	Snack
Cereal, banana	Hamburger and roll	Pasta with veg-	Chocolate cake
2% milk	French fries	etables and	2% milk
Toast and jam	Carrot-raisin salad	Parmesan cheese	
Orange juice	V-8 juice	Whole wheat rolls	
	2% milk	2% milk	
		Fruit bowl	

| Breakfast | Thursday—afternoon game | | Snack |
	Lunch	Dinner	
Cream-of-Wheat	Tuna sandwich	2 hamburgers	Chocolate chip
Toast and jam	Tomato soup	Salad	cookies
Strawberries	Crackers	Vanilla shake	2% milk
Orange juice	Coleslaw		Popcorn, lemonade
	2% milk		
	Fruit jello		

| Breakfast | Friday | | Snack |
	Lunch	Dinner	
Blueberries and	Mexican salad	Shrimp and pasta	Melon and
waffles	Corn bread	Salad	pineapple
Syrup	Peaches	Whole wheat rolls	chunks
2% milk	2% milk	2% milk	Lemonade
Orange juice	Sherbet	Strawberry pie	

Breakfast	Saturday—all-day tournament Snacks between games	Fast-food dinner
Pancakes	Peanut butter on crackers	Pasta salad bar
Syrup	Oyster or graham crackers	Rolls
Orange juice	Apples, oranges, bananas	Hamburger
Muffins	Rolls, bagels	Vanilla shake

Brunch	Sunday Dinner	Snack
Scrambled eggs,	V-8 juice	Popcorn
ham	Roast beef	
4 pieces toast with	Potato	
jam	Salad	
Fruit cup	Peas and onions	
Orange and tomato	Rolls	
juice	Angel food cake	
2% milk	2% milk	

Table 6.9
Nutrition Checklist

	Mon	Tues	Wed	Thurs	Fri	Sat	Sun	Goals
How many servings of *grain* did I have today?								9
How many servings of *milk* did I have today?								3 to 4
How many servings of *fruits* and *vegetables* did I have today?								minimum of 5
How many ounces of *meat* did I have today?								5 to 6
How many cups of water did I have today?								8

The Nutrition Checklist

A good way for each of your players to find out whether his diet is up to par is by filling out a nutrition checklist. Give all your players copies of the checklist in Table 6.9 and encourage them to fill them out each night for 1 week. Along with the checklist, give each a copy of the food groups in Table 6.5. This is a good way for them to learn about the makeup of foods as well as their own food habits.

Packing a Travel Cooler

A good one-time investment for your team is a cooler. You can take it on the road or use it at home to keep water and juices chilled (remember, cold water is absorbed faster than water at room temperature). Here are some other suggestions for cooler items, especially for away games:

Fresh fruit

Fruit juices in individual boxes

Water

Jar of peanut butter (don't forget a knife)

3 boxes of wheat crackers

3 bags of pretzels

Box of graham crackers

A Healthy Fast-Food Eating Guide

Eating on the road can be tough on the budget, so most teams stop at fast-food chains. Nutritionally speaking, this can be a real challenge. Two

Table 6.10
Healthy Fast-Food Choices

McDonald's regular hamburger or cheeseburger (not a Big Mac), salad, shake, sundae

Wendy's plain baked potato, chili, chicken breast fillet sandwich, single hamburger, salad

Pizza Hut thick-crust pizza—easy on the meat and cheese!

Kentucky Fried Chicken original-recipe chicken breast, corn-on-the-cob, mashed potatoes

Taco Bell bean burrito, tostada, combination burrito

Long John Silver's coleslaw, ocean scallops, shrimp with batter, breaded oysters

problems with fast foods are their high fat content and their lack of fruits and vegetables. But salad bars, low-fat milk, and self-styled hamburgers have helped the nutritional standing of many fast-food chains.

Table 6.10 is a list of some major fast-food chains and suggestions for healthy food choices.

What to Eat Before, During, and After Games

Pregame meals, whatever the time of day they are eaten, should be satisfying but kept light. Two sample breakfast meals are (a) cereal, 2% milk, whole wheat toast with jam, and orange juice, or (b) pancakes with syrup, 2% milk, and orange juice.

Two sample lunch or supper menus are (a) turkey sandwich, crackers, pickles, apple, and 2% milk, or (b) spaghetti, bread, 2% milk, banana, and fruit jello.

During a game, players should drink plenty of water. Between games, players should snack on crackers, apples, oranges, bananas, rolls, and bagels (Table 6.11).

Table 6.11
Between-Game Eating

Yes	No
Peanut butter crackers	Soft drinks
Oranges, apples, bananas	Candy bars
Crackers	Sugary fruit juice
Diluted fruit juice	Deluxe hamburgers
Pretzels	French fries
Bagels	Potato chips
Water	

After the game, glycogen should be restored with a high-carbohydrate meal such as spaghetti and meat sauce, a thick-crust pizza, or pancakes with syrup.

KEYS TO SUCCESS

- Your nutrition knowledge can make a big difference to your team's performance—pass it on!
- A high-carbohydrate diet during the season means high-energy performance.
- Muscle glycogen stores are used up by hard ballplaying, and they can only be replaced by food carbohydrates.
- Carbohydrates can be complex (starch) as in bread, pasta, rice, and beans, or simple (sugar) as in carrots, candy, yogurt, fruit, soft drinks, and milk. Players should choose more complex carbohydrates than simple ones.
- Your players should eat plenty of complex carbohydrates every day, not just the night before a game.
- Have your players balance their diets by choosing from the six food groups—meat, milk, grain, fruit, vegetable, and fat.
- Encourage your players to eat three meals a day, plus snacks, rather than skip meals. Their energy levels will be much more constant.
- Pregame meals should be eaten at least 3 hours before game time.
- Avoid simple carbohydrates the hour before game time.
- If hunger strikes before or between games, eat pretzels, crackers, and fruit and drink water.
- Be sure your players drink plenty of cool water, especially on hot, humid days.

RESOURCES

American Dietetics Association
216 W. Jackson Blvd., Suite 800
Chicago, IL 60606-6995
1-800-877-1600
Ext.-4852 for Department of Nutrition Resources, for nutrition guidelines
   and pamphlets
Ext.-4841 for Membership Department, for programs
Ext.-4893 for Policy Administration, for state or local nutrition contacts

Acknowledgments
Special thanks to Dave Wright, coach of Towson Senior High School's baseball team, and Mike Gottlieb, coach of Towson State University's baseball team, both in Maryland, for their helpful insights and discussion.

Index

About the Editor & Authors

Editor

In 1956, **Jerry Kindall** signed a bonus contract with the Chicago Cubs. He played as infielder for eight years in the Big Leagues with the Cubs, Cleveland Indians, and Minnesota Twins. He was with the 1965 American League Champion Twins his last year before retiring from professional baseball. He next joined the University of Minnesota Athletic Staff from 1966 to 1972. While there, he received his M.A. in physical education. His next move was to the University of Arizona.

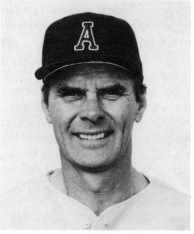

Jerry has been Head Baseball Coach at the University of Arizona since 1972, giving him the honor of being the coach with the longest term of service at Arizona. Under his direction, Arizona has been an NCAA regional finalist nine years, has advanced to the NCAA College World Series in Omaha five times, and has been the NCAA Champion in 1976, 1980, and 1986. Jerry has been named NCAA College Baseball Coach of the Year three times, PAC-6 Coach of the Year twice, and was Sporting News College Coach of the Year in 1980. He was inducted into the College Baseball Coaches Hall of Fame in 1991.

Jerry, a widower, married Diane Sargent, also widowed, in 1988. Jerry's four married children from his previous marriage are Betsy, Doug, Bruce, and Martha. Diane's two children are Rodney and Elisa.

Authors

Craig A. Wrisberg grew up in St. Louis where he learned to love the game of baseball. His background in physical education includes a B.A. from Greenville College and an M.A. from Indiana State University. He then received an M.A. in psychology and a Ph.D. in motor behavior at the University of Michigan. Dr. Wrisberg is currently a professor in the Department of Human Performance and Sport Studies at the University of Tennessee at Knoxville, teaching courses and conducting research in motor learning and control, and applied  sport psychology. He also serves as a sport psychological consultant for the Men's Athletic Department. Dr. Wrisberg is a Fellow of the American Academy of Physical Education and of the Research Consortium of the American Alliance for Health, Physical Education, Recreation and Dance. He has served as President of the North American Society for the Psychology of Sport and Physical Activity.

Tom Hanson is Head Baseball Coach at Skidmore College in Saratoga Springs, New York and a member of the Physical Education and Dance faculty, teaching courses in the sports studies curriculum. As an undergraduate at Luther College in Iowa, his baseball team won three conference championships and Tom gained all-conference honors. He was a graduate assistant baseball coach while working for his Masters at the University of Illinois at Urbana-Champaign, and an assistant baseball coach while pursuing his Ph.D. in sport psychology at  the University of Virginia. Dr. Hanson's research interests include stress management and coach/athlete relationships. For his doctoral dissertation, he conducted a qualitative study on the mental aspects of hitting, which is based on his personal interviews with many all-time hitting greats. Dr. Hanson is also a member of the Association for the Advancement of Applied Sport Psychology.

Lois A. Klatt is the director of the Human Performance Laboratory, a professor of Human Performance, and an advisor of the Exercise Science and Fitness Management Program at Concordia University in River Forest, Illinois. Dr. Klatt received a B.A. in physical education at West Chester State University in Pennsylvania and did graduate work in biomechanics, receiving an M.S. from the University of Wisconsin at Madison, and a Ph.D. from the University of Indiana at Bloomington. She is currently a research consultant for the Chicago  White Sox and has done much work on injury prevention with numerous organizations such as the Chicago Bears and the United States Olympic Committee. Dr. Klatt's involvement with professional organizations is extensive and includes the American Alliance for Health, Physical Education, Recreation and Dance; American College of Sports Medicine; Biomechanic Association of the USA; and the International Society of Biomechanics in Sports.

Coop DeRenne is an associate professor in the Department of Health, Physical Education, and Recreation at the University of Hawaii at Manoa. He received a B.A. from California State University at Northridge, an M.S. from the University of Southern California at Los Angeles, and an Ed.D. from Brigham Young University. Dr. DeRenne has taught at elementary, junior high, and high schools. He has coached at Hawaii high schools and as assistant coach at the University of Hawaii. He played and then became  a professional scout for the Montreal Expos Organization. He later was a research consultant for the Texas Rangers and also for the Chicago White Sox Organization, where he was also Minor League Coach. Dr. DeRenne has been a member of the American College of Sports Medicine; American Sports Medicine Institute; American Alliance for Health, Physical Education, Recreation and Dance; Athletic Orthopedic Institute; and National Strength and Conditioning Association.

Herbert K. Amato is the Curriculum Director for Athletic Training at James Madison University, in Harrisonburg, Virginia. His educational background in Physical Education includes a B.S. from West Virginia University, and an M.S. Ed. from James Madison University. He is pursuing a D.A. from Middle Tennessee State University. Mr. Amato is a member of the National Athletic Trainers' Association and serves as a member of the Executive Council of the Virginia Athletic Trainers' Association. He previously worked as head athletic trainer at the high school and college levels and has been an active speaker on drug testing, anabolic steroid use, and the prevention of throwing injuries throughout the Mid-Atlantic Area. Mr. Amato worked six summers as an athletic trainer for the United States Olympic Committee and worked with the U.S.A. Baseball team in 1988, concluding with the summer Olympics in Seoul, South Korea.

Gale Beliveau Carey, M.S., Ph.D., L.N. is an Assistant Professor in the Human Nutrition Program of Animal and Nutrition Sciences at the University of New Hampshire in Durham. She is a member of the American Institute of Nutrition, American Nutritionists Association, American Dietetics Association, and the American College of Sports Medicine. Her education in Biochemistry and nutritional sciences allows her to conduct extensive research in intermediary metabolism. She has also studied the nutrition and performance of the University of New Hampshire swim and crew teams. Dr. Carey opted for a career in science by default at age 13 when she realized that she would never play first base for the Boston Red Sox. Her interest in sports continues. She is a long-distance runner, veteran of five marathons (including Boston) and innumerable middle distance events, an avid baseball fan, and a loyal baseball scorekeeper for the Chicago-based STATS, Inc.